The Nature of Recreation   **A handbook in honor of Frederick Law Olmsted, using examples from his work**

Richard Saul Wurman
Alan Levy
Joel Katz

of GEE! Group for Environmental
Education Inc.
with Jean McClintock
and Howard Brunner

Copyright © 1972 by
The American Federation of Arts
and GEE! Group for Environmental
Education Inc.

Library of Congress catalog card
number
GV182.2.G7   790'.013   72-8898
ISBN 0-262-23063-1
ISBN 0-262-73034-0 (pbk.)

Published by the MIT Press,
Cambridge, Massachusetts, and
London, England, for
The American Federation of Arts,
and made possible by a grant
from the Rockefeller Brothers
Fund.

The American Federation of Arts
41 East 65 Street
New York, New York 10021

GEE! Group for Environmental
Education Inc.
1214 Arch Street
Philadelphia, Pennsylvania 19107

Preface

This handbook is a response to the sesquicentennial celebration of the birth of Frederick Law Olmsted. It is published on the occasion of exhibitions on Olmsted developed at the National Gallery of Art and the Whitney Museum of American Art. This format carries with it a suggested avenue for future museum catalogues, encouraging participation with the contents of an exhibition.

Enlarging our ability to communicate our recreational needs and desires is a subject that demands our collective advocacy.

We have attempted to help the reader learn to articulate constructive demands for recreation and for recreational facilities. Our tribute to Frederick Law Olmsted uses his works and words as a beginning point for this handbook-long definition of the nature of recreation. And we have attempted a meeting and an embrace between the performances of recreation and the physical places and spaces such performances desire to occupy.

We have had a lot of help. Although we have listed our gratitude in detail at the back of the book, it seems appropriate to acknowledge specially Harold Snedcof of the Rockefeller Brothers Fund who allowed this book birth by his matching some of our ideas about education to the Olmsted sesquicentennial year.

At best, this book will help you see some things that you have always seen but never seen.

Contents

4 **The Nature of Recreation**
5 Introduction
5 Frederick Law Olmsted
8 What Did You Do Last Year?
What Would You Like to Have Done?

What You Will Find in This Book

We have designed this book with three different kinds of type and three different kinds of illustration so that you can follow the line or lines of development that you find most interesting.

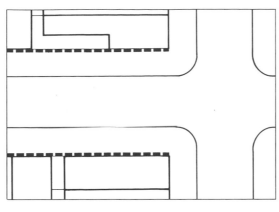

10 **Our Recreational Needs**

16 **Identifying Our Needs by Performance Components**

18 What is Performance?

20 Inactive/Active

22 Individual/Group

24 Young/Old

26 Specific/Nonspecific

28 Small/Large

30 Linear/Nonlinear

32 Flat/Sloped

34 Access and Distribution

36 Movement

38 Safety and Comfort

40 Time, Temperature, Weather

42 Preservation and Construction

44 Maintenance

46 **Working with Performance**

46 Analyzing Activities by Performance Components

48 Locating Your Recreational Resources

50 Analyzing One of Your Recreational Resources

52 Developing a Program

54 Identifying Recreational Possibilities

56 Choosing among Recreational Possibilities

60 Developing Recreational Resources

65 Afterword

65 **Appendix**

65 An Olmsted Bibliography

66 A Recreational Bibliography

71 The Street

72 A Game Glossary

74 Game Spaces

76 Credits and Acknowledgments

The basic text of the book is printed in this kind of type. In this text you will find a general discussion of recreational needs and performance components and captions for all the photographs. Also in this section are projects and exercises for you to do to develop and evaluate your own ideas about recreation. The photographs and plans printed in black ink accompany this text; most of them are of recreational areas designed by Olmsted. At the end of the book is an appendix which includes bibliographies, quotations, and games.

The text set in this type and the photographs printed in brown deal with the times and writings of Frederick Law Olmsted. This text includes a brief biography of Olmsted and selections from his writings. All the photographs and plans printed in brown date from the nineteenth century.

In the margin of the page are illustrations and text in small type, which form a running appendix of interesting pieces of information. It is hoped that this part of the book will give you a wide range of recreational information and entertain you.

The Nature of Recreation

The need for recreation is universal. Whether you spend most of your day in school, at work, or at home, and whether you live in the city, the suburbs, or the country, you share this universal need. Your idea of recreation may be playing a sport or watching it on television, sitting under a tree, sailing a boat—or all of these —but far from being a luxury in your life, recreation is a necessity.

Even in the few examples above, it is clear that recreation takes place both outdoors and indoors, in public and in private; our recreational needs could not be filled without the inclusion of outdoor-public, outdoor-private, indoor-public, and indoor-private opportunities. But as more and more meadows sprout high-rise apartments and sprawling subdivisions, and as trees with seeming inevitability make way for roads, it appears that the public outdoor aspect of recreation is most in danger of not meeting our present and future needs.

Public outdoor recreation is the subject of this book. Its title, *The Nature of Recreation,* was chosen because of the importance of both *nature* and *recreation.* The word *nature* emphasizes the importance of the natural environment in recreational planning and enjoyment. And the root of *recreation* is *re-creation,* our ability to refresh and renew ourselves.

The intention of *The Nature of Recreation* is to help us increase our knowledge about what outdoor public recreation really means to us, to give us a framework to identify and articulate our needs, and to encourage us to form a wider understanding of our existing and potential recreational resources. How to make the resources we have work better for us is the challenge that recreational planning faces, a challenge that you can help meet.

Our present understanding of outdoor public recreation owes a great debt to the work and writings of Frederick Law Olmsted (1822-1903), to whom this handbook is dedicated. Olmsted was one of the first Americans to be actively and professionally concerned with finding —and when it couldn't be found, making —outdoor public recreational space.

As real estate speculators increasingly viewed America's undeveloped land only as a place to build on, Olmsted saw it as a place *not* to build on. Central Park—the first public park of Olmsted's career and the first attempt anywhere to translate democratic social ideals into a recreational land use plan—provides a perfect example. Even when New York City's northern boundary of intensely urban development was Fourteenth Street, Olmsted anticipated the need for balance between the urban and natural worlds.

Believing that no room would be left for the outdoor public sphere of man's life, Olmsted created places for athletic sports, for strolling, for public gatherings, and generally for relief from the hard monotony of tall buildings and crowded streets. In 1857-58 Olmsted and his partner, the English-born architect Calvert Vaux, designed a central park for New York, which they called "Greensward."

Introduction

Frederick Law Olmsted

Olmsted about 1860.

During the 81 years of his life, Frederick Law Olmsted tried many professions: clerk, cabin boy, farmer, writer, journalist, traveler, editor, politician, government official, and landscape architect, the profession he created. This variety of experience contributed to his understanding of his time, which he translated into projects to meet future urban needs.

Olmsted regarded his childhood as instrumental in awakening his later interest in making the natural environment a component of the expanding urban one. Born in Hartford, Connecticut, in 1822, by the time he was 14 Olmsted had lived and studied with rural preachers and explored the New England countryside around their homes. While his friends were entering college (which he was advised against because of temporarily weak vision), Olmsted took up what he called "a decently restrained vagabond life," in the course of which he attended lectures at Yale for a year.

The park became a model for meeting the recreational needs of a city and providing a balance between the environment of urban structures and the natural world. It advanced the radical idea that land must be left open—open from construction and open for people.

Through conversations, lectures, reports, and by the example of his work, Olmsted reminded people of their need for open

When he was 24, Olmsted joined the crew of a ship sailing to China; upon his return, he apprenticed himself to two farmers. In 1848, his father bought him a farm on Staten Island, where he was able to try out his ideas about farming on a small scale. After two years, his desire for travel resurfacing, he embarked on a tour of England with his brother. Impressed by English rural life and fascinated by the planning and construction of deceptively natural park landscapes, he wrote Walks and Talks of an American Farmer in England, *which was published in 1852.*

The book's success led the New York Daily Times *to commission a series of articles on conditions in the South. His observations (eventually collected into one volume,* The Cotton Kingdom, *published in 1861) are distinguished by their sensitivity and attention to detail. They reveal Olmsted's awareness of the connection between cultural traditions and economic conditions on the one hand and political and social conditions on the other.*

Fifth Avenue at Ninety-third Street in New York City, at the edge of Central Park, in Olmsted's day and in 1972.

"I had not been aware that the park was such a nasty place. In fact, the low grounds were steeped in the overflow and mush of pig-sties, slaughter-houses, and bone-boiling works, and the stench was sickening."
Letter to John Olmsted, 1857.

In 1858, Olmsted and English-born Calvert Vaux won the competition for a major park design for New York City with their plan "Greensward," and in that year Olmsted was appointed architect-in-chief of the park. Largely completed by 1861, Central Park was, from the beginning, an appropriate realization of Olmsted's knowledge of soils and agriculture, his social convictions and commitments, and his understanding of the environmental and recreational needs of the city-dweller.

With the almost immediate success of Central Park, Olmsted's talents were much in demand by other cities interested in following New York's example. But in 1861, Olmsted volunteered as executive secretary of the U.S. Sanitary Commission, precursor of the American

space, and he translated his personal perception and concern into a public awareness and political force comparable to our present concern for the environment. At the close of the nineteenth century the people to whom Olmsted's message spread planted trees bordering the streets, built city squares, public gardens, playgrounds, small neighborhood and larger city parks, and created vast wilderness preserves.

In the course of his prolific career, Olmsted designed at least thirty-seven urban parks (seventeen of them large area parks), sixteen suburban plans, fourteen campuses, three conservation areas, one regional system of parks, plus the grounds of numerous private estates and institutions. Neither his works nor his words give us all the answers to our recreational needs and problems. Our intellectual stance and our social fabric have changed too much. His work and words are presented here to reveal the man and his particular genius.

But in this 150th year of Olmsted's birth, when our recreational spaces face the challenges of a burgeoning population, the vast increase in leisure time, and changing individual and social values, we have much to learn from Olmsted, not only from his work as a landscape architect and environmentalist, but particularly from his work as a recreational theorist. His methodology—basing his solutions on a rigorous analysis of social patterns and a true respect for and understanding of human needs—is as applicable today as then. We can think of no better way to honor him than to help make *the nature of recreation* more understandable so that each of us can take part in the decisions that will shape our recreational future.

Red Cross. After working himself virtually to exhaustion, he accepted the directorship of the Mariposa Mining Estates in California. While there, he studied the site for the University of California at Berkeley and proposed the creation of a national park in the Yosemite Valley.

In 1865, at the urging of Vaux and lured by the opportunity of working on Prospect Park in Brooklyn and on the weekly review, The Nation, *Olmsted returned to New York to take up officially a career as a landscape architect. Repeatedly frustrated by political interference and bureaucratic stupidity, and after several resignations and reappointments, Olmsted transferred the major part of his energy from New York to Boston, and moved permanently to Brookline in 1883. The Boston period of his career, which began in the late 1870's, included work in Montreal, the Biltmore estate, and the World's Columbian Exposition in Chicago.*

In 1895, Olmsted retired from professional practice and visited England. Later in the year he was institutionalized as the result of a nervous breakdown, and in August 1903 he died at the McLean Asylum, which he had landscaped, in Waverly, Massachusetts.

Olmsted about 1885.

Selected Projects by Frederick Law Olmsted
Central, Riverside, and Morningside Parks, New York City. Prospect and Fort Green Parks, Brooklyn. Amusement resort, Rockaway Point, New York. South Park and Jackson Park, Chicago. Franklin and Wood Island Parks, and Charlestown Playground, Boston. National Zoo, Washington, D.C. Parks for Albany, Buffalo, Rochester, San Francisco, Newark, Philadelphia, Montreal, Detroit, Hartford, Trenton, Louisville, Milwaukee, Kansas City.

Riverside, near Chicago. Suburbs and subdivisions in Newark, Providence, Newport, Brookline, Buffalo, Baltimore, Atlanta

The Biltmore Estate for George Vanderbilt, Ashville, North Carolina.

World's Columbian Exposition, 1893, Chicago.

Institutional landscaping in Boston (Massachusetts General Hospital), Syracuse, Hartford (State Capitol grounds), Philadelphia, Albany, Buffalo, Washington, D.C. (Capitol grounds).

Campus planning for Amherst, Trinity, Yale, Johns Hopkins, Colgate, Smith, Harvard, Stanford, U.S. Military Academy.

Conservation works at Mariposa Mining Estates, Yosemite and Mariposa Big Tree Groves, and Niagara Falls.

The Boston park system.

What Did You Do Last Year?

There are two ways of ranking recreational activities in order of popularity: one is by the number of people—the percentage of the population—who engage in them; the other is to rank how often each activity is pursued. The difference between the two sets of results indicates that many activities experienced by large numbers of people are done so only infrequently, while other activities experienced by smaller numbers of people are done so with much greater frequency.

Below are the most popular outdoor activities in terms of the percentage of the population engaging in each one at least once in 1965, measured by the U.S. Department of the Interior.

Picnicking	57%
Sightseeing	49%
Swimming	48%
Walking for pleasure	48%
Outdoor sports	33%
Fishing	30%
Watching sports events	30%
Boating	24%
Bicycling	16%
Nature walks	14%
Sledding	13%
Hunting	12%
Attending an outdoor concert or play	11%
Camping	10%
Ice skating	9%
Horseback riding	8%
Hiking	7%
Waterskiing	6%
Skiing	4%
Canoeing	3%
Sailing	3%

Below are two identical checklists. Both lists contain 96 things that you can do outdoors. In the top checklist fill in the circle for each recreational activity you did during the past year. Then fill in the circles in the bottom checklist for everything you would like to have done outdoors last year. You will then be able to examine how much you are actually using the outdoors for recreation (by looking at the top list); how much you would like to take advantage of the outdoors for recreation (by looking at the bottom list); and how close you are to taking as much advantage of the outdoors for recreation as you would like (by comparing the two lists).

What Would You Like to Have Done?

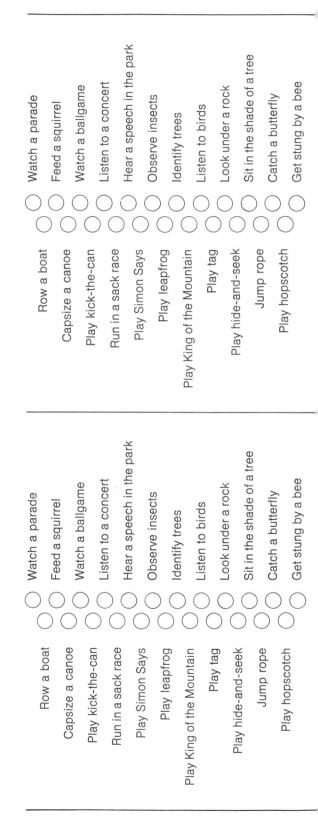

Activity checklist (upper)

Twirl a hula-hoop · Catch poison ivy · Build a snowman · Go to a fair · Build a sand castle · Wrestle · Camp out · Do push-ups · Sit in a treehouse · Nap in the grass · Have a picnic · Daydream · Swing · Have a chat on a bench · Slide · Play blindman's bluff · See-saw · Shoot marbles · Have a tug-of-war · Climb on a jungle gym · Play house · Climb a tree · Play cowboys and Indians · Play ping-pong · Play croquet · Play baseball · Play bocce · Play football · Play handball · Play golf · Catch a frisbee · Play basketball · Play badminton · Play volleyball · Throw horseshoes · Play tennis · Play shuffleboard · Play soccer · Ski · Swim · Sled · Skin dive · Ride a horse · Wade in the water · Skate on a skateboard · Catch a fish · Iceskate · Feed a duck · Climb a hill · Skip rocks · Roll down a hill · Lawn bowl · Backpack · Fly a kite · Watch boats on a river · Surf · Look for wildflowers · Waterski · Find wild animal tracks · Pick up seashells · Rollerskate · Play cards in the grass · Ride a bike · Play chess · Jog · Play a guitar under a tree · Walk in the park · Paint a picture · Walk a dog · Write poetry · Sail a boat · Sit by a lake · Sunbathe at the beach

Activity checklist (lower)

Twirl a hula-hoop · Catch poison ivy · Build a snowman · Go to a fair · Build a sand castle · Wrestle · Camp out · Do push-ups · Sit in a treehouse · Nap in the grass · Have a picnic · Daydream · Swing · Have a chat on a bench · Slide · Play blindman's bluff · See-saw · Shoot marbles · Have a tug-of-war · Climb on a jungle gym · Play house · Climb a tree · Play cowboys and Indians · Play ping-pong · Play croquet · Play baseball · Play bocce · Play football · Play handball · Play golf · Catch a frisbee · Play basketball · Play badminton · Play volleyball · Throw horseshoes · Play tennis · Play shuffleboard · Play soccer · Ski · Swim · Sled · Skin dive · Ride a horse · Wade in the water · Skate on a skateboard · Catch a fish · Iceskate · Feed a duck · Climb a hill · Skip rocks · Roll down a hill · Lawn bowl · Backpack · Fly a kite · Watch boats on a river · Surf · Look for wildflowers · Waterski · Find wild animal tracks · Pick up seashells · Rollerskate · Play cards in the grass · Ride a bike · Play chess · Jog · Play a guitar under a tree · Walk in the park · Paint a picture · Walk a dog · Write poetry · Sail a boat · Sit by a lake · Sunbathe at the beach

More Activity Statistics

Following is a ranking of activities by the total number of times each was experienced during 1965. You will see that the ranking is quite different than when the activities were ranked by the percentage of the population participating in them.

Walking for pleasure
Swimming
Driving for pleasure
Playing outdoor games
Bicycling
Sightseeing
Picnicking
Fishing
Attending outdoor games
Boating
Nature walks
Camping
Horseback riding
Waterskiing
Hiking
Attending outdoor plays and concerts

The five outdoor activities which are experienced the greatest number of times in a year, on the average, by the people participating in them, are, in order:

Bicycling
Playing outdoor games
Walking for pleasure
Swimming
Driving for pleasure

How much use these statistics are in calculating future recreational needs is the subject of some debate. In *Outdoor Recreation Trends,* the formula relies heavily on projecting current trends and the expected increases in population, affluence, and leisure time. Many writers, however, dispute this system, anticipating a decisive influence of future technology which cannot presently be calculated.

Our Recreational Needs

Leisure
As the amount of leisure time for workers increases so will our need for space and facilities to accommodate recreational activity. In the 1870's, the average work week was about 53 hours. Today, the average is close to 40 hours, 13 hours less than a century ago. Increased leisure time comes from reductions in the work week, longer vacations, more holidays, greater opportunities for part-time work, the shift away from farming, and a longer life expectancy. (From 1900 to 1960, life expectancy increased by 18 years while working life expectancy increased by nine. This represents a nine year increase in leisure time.)

The 40-hour work week represents a gain of 675 hours of free time annually over the last century. Vacation time gains add another 70 hours and holidays account for an additional 45 hours. This means that the total gain of free time since the 1870's has been roughly one month out of every twelve. When the nonworking years of youth and retirement are added to this, the total leisure hours in the average man's life approaches 50,000.

Leisure time will continue to grow in the future but people will prefer longer vacations, longer weekends, and earlier retirement rather than free hours added to the work day.

Are you surprised by the number of things you would like to have done outdoors last year but didn't do? Why didn't you do them? Perhaps you just didn't have time. Perhaps a few activities were too expensive. But how many things didn't you do simply because there wasn't the opportunity near enough or convenient enough for you?

Have you ever considered how important being outside really is? Somehow throwing a ball around, having a picnic, or walking alone along a wooded path provide a necessary and satisfying change from the things we usually do and the places where we spend most of our time. Walking through a meadow or sitting under a tree at the edge of a lake does something for us that walking to school or work or sitting in our own backyard just can't do.

We all desire these nonroutine experiences because recreation satisfies basic human needs that are as important as eating or sleeping. We need the exhaustion and exuberance of exercise; the company of friends, acquaintances, and just other people; the regenerative effects of solitude; and the change in our environment and the opportunity for learning that recreation, particularly outdoor recreation, provides. Recreation allows us to step out of our customary lives and, by engaging ourselves in what we most want to do, to rediscover and re-create ourselves.

"We want a ground to which people may easily go after their day's work is done, and where they may stroll for an hour, seeing, hearing, and feeling nothing of the bustle and jar of the streets, where they shall, in effect, find the city put far away from them. We want the greatest possible contrast with the streets and the shops and the rooms of the town which will be consistent with convenience and the preservation of good order and neatness. We want, especially, the greatest possible contrast with the restraining and confining conditions which compel us to walk circumspectly, watchfully, jealously, which compel us to look closely upon others without sympathy. Practically, what we most want is a simple, broad, open space of clean greensward, with sufficient play of surface and a sufficient number of trees about it to supply a variety of light and shade. This we want as a central feature. We want depth of wood enough about it not only for comfort in hot weather, but to completely shut out the city from our landscapes."
Public Parks and the Enlargement of Towns,
1870.

The Henry Street Settlement in New York, about 1898.

Many people think of recreation in terms of strenuous physical exercise, whether it's the bruising contact of a sport like football, the sociable exhilaration of swimming or sledding, or the private satisfaction of jogging alone in the morning mist. Recreation in its physical form includes all such activities and more, and its benefits extend far beyond physical health. Children, for example, use as much mental as physical energy in playing cowboys and Indians.

In all cases physical recreation offers experiences that we don't encounter in our daily routines and provides an outlet for energies left unused at the end of an ordinary day. The special challenge of physical competition and the importance of exercise have long been recognized: the Olympic games, which accord honor to physical achievement, were begun by the Greeks more than 2500 years ago.

Much of our outdoor recreational space today is devoted to playing fields for various games and sports. In addition to answering our needs for exercise, these large public spaces remind us how much of our recreational activity, strenuous or not, involves other people.

"If a considerable number of people of the city were impressed with the importance of out-of-door exercise for themselves and their children . . . [they] would . . . provide the opportunities for it at their own cost and charges."
Tenth Annual Report on Central Park, 1886.

To meet the particular needs of one Brooklyn neighborhood, Olmsted designed Fort Green Park with turf prepared for children's play areas encircled with wooded paths for strolling.

The Olympics
The Olympic games were the most notable of the four Pan-hellenic festivals (the others were the Isthmian, Nemean, and Pythian). Held every four years in the first month of the summer solstice, they began in 776 B.C. The Greeks adopted this date as the first year in their chronology. A general peace was maintained throughout the festival and for one week before and after the games.

Typical game events included foot races, discus and javelin throwing, wrestling, boxing, horse and chariot racing, and the pankration, a combination of wrestling and boxing. The victor's prize was a crown of wild olive, a palm branch, and the right to erect a statue in the Altis, the central enclosure of the sacred temple precincts. Zeus was the chief deity to whom the festival was dedicated. The modern era of the Olympic games began in Athens in 1896.

As long as people have grouped together, first in small communities and later in towns and huge cities, outdoor public spaces designed for large congregations of people have existed. The agora in every Greek city provided an identifiable place for people of differing backgrounds from anywhere in the region to meet and exchange ideas as well as money and merchandise. Public baths have been social centers from the days of ancient Rome to contemporary Japan. No Italian Renaissance city was built without its piazzas, and no colonial New England village was laid out without a common green, almost always in the center of the town. Today our socializing has become less formal and official, more casual, but we are still concerned with providing ways to be among other people—to watch, to be watched, to meet and interact. The outdoor cafe, the public urban park, the rock concert, and the street are among today's equivalents of yesterday's agoras, baths, and squares—clearly identifiable places to meet, talk, and be among people.

The agora in ancient Athens, public baths throughout the Roman Empire, the Italian piazza, and the New England village common were created to fill the need for socializing in their day.

"I have never been long in any locality . . . without observing a custom of gregarious out-of-door recreation in some miserably imperfect form. . . . I am sure that it would be much better . . . if it were admitted to be a distinct requirement of all human beings, and appropriately provided for."
Public Parks and the Enlargement of Towns.

Bethesda Terrace and Fountain in Central Park, in the 1860's and today. The gondolas were a gift to the City of New York from Venice.

Most of us find the break from routine
that recreation provides makes us better
able to enjoy our work when we resume it.
In the same way, our enjoyment of other
people is increased by the time we spend
alone. Have you ever thought about how
tedious life would be if you could never
be alone? Jean-Paul Sartre defined hell
as "other people" without relief. When
we are alone, we are free to be ourselves,
to let our imaginations roam, to remember, to dream, or to make plans.

Three-fourths of the people in this country
live in cities, which every day become
dirtier, more crowded, and more dangerous. It seems natural, then, that we enjoy
being alone from time to time, away from
our responsibilities and the watchful eyes
of other people. And it is understandable
that our solitude can be enhanced by the
vastness and restfulness of nature, the
coolness of water, the shade of a tree, and
the softness of grass trembling in a breeze.

Olmsted and his wife in
Yosemite, whose *"distinctive
charm lies in the rare association with the grandeur of
its rocky elements, of brooks
flowing quietly through the
ferny and bosky glades of
very beautifully disposed
great bodies, groups, and
clusters of trees."*

Trees as Education
The golden larch is one of over 118 beautiful and rare tree and shrub varieties gathered in Central Park from throughout the world. It can be seen on a walking tour of the park near lamppost 8529, near 85th Street and Central Park West. The cones of the golden larch provide the clue necessary to distinguish it from other pine varieties. They are large and fleshy and as they ripen fall apart shedding both seeds and scales together. In the process of drying, the scale uncovers two winged seeds which are cupped like the blade of a pinwheel. These cones may be seen near the top of the tree. In early summer, the brown tassels of male flowers are conspicuous on the lower branches. This placement (seen also in pines, alders, birches, and other wind pollinated trees) is an ingenious device to avoid self-pollination. The needle arrangement of golden larches is in whorls, creating a saucer-like effect of radiating needles.

Did you ever throw yourself down on a patch of grass and observe the infinite variety of life right before you? Did you notice the intense activities of insects, the sunlight and shadow on one blade of grass, the intricate veining on a leaf dropped from a nearby tree?

The most direct way to learn is by experience. We learn about cars, traffic lights, and road construction by seeing them in our urban environment and we learn about trees, birds, and flowers by exploring them in their natural environment. No matter how much we read about the seasons, we learn to understand spring by watching the delicate green buds grow a little bigger and darker each day, and to associate autumn with the deeply colored leaves we walk through on the way to school or work.

What we learn by observation and in response to our curiosity is remembered with particular intensity because we discovered it ourselves. The places where this kind of education can best take place—our parks, zoos, wildlife preserves, and national forests—are the best kind of classrooms we can build for our natural world. They are classrooms that we will never get tired of—even the path we explored last week will have become a little different by today.

"You can hardly fail to see wherein the advantage of the property lies, as an educative and civilizing agency, standing in winning competition against the sordid and corrupting temptations of the town. You can hardly fail to realize how much greater wealth it thus places within your reach than is to be found in the ordinary parks and gardens, not to say the museums and galleries, which are the pride of other cities, and which millions have been thriftily expended to obtain...."
Mount Royal.

The conservatory in Prospect Park in Brooklyn, New York. Olmsted was concerned with enlarging the scope of plant variety, and in all his work he made an effort to include trees, shrubs, and flowers from far-away places with similar climatic conditions to those of his site.

"In its influence as an educator, as a place of agreeable resort, as a source of scientific interest, and in its effect upon the health, happiness, and comfort of our people may be found its chief value."
Report of the Commissioners of Central Park, 1870.

15

STEREO-TRAVEL CO. STEREO-TRAVEL CO.

THE GLOBE STEREOGRAPH CO. CHICAGO THE GLOBE STEREOGRAPH CO. CHICAGO

81. Children in Central Park.
Copyright, 1909, by Stereo-Travel Co.

166—Lunching in Central Park, New York.
Copyright, 1906, by the Globe Stereograph Co.

Lawn Tennis in Central Park N.Y.

249.

249

A. S. CAMPBELL ELIZABETH, N. J.

Alfred S. Campbell

Copyrighted 1896
By ALFRED S. CAMPBELL,
ELIZABETH, N. J., U. S. A.

357—Bicycling, Central Park, N.Y.

Underwood & Underwood, Publishers.
New York, London, Toronto Canada, Ottawa Kansas

Lover's Lane, Central Park, New York.
Copyright 1896 by, Strohmeyer & Wyman.

122.

Swan Boats, Central Park, N.Y.

Jan 1896

122

A. S. CAMPBELL, ELIZABETH, N. J.

What Is Performance?

The process of determining our recreational needs is a very difficult one for we have to take account of the wide range of needs that any group of individuals will have. (Obviously not everyone likes to exercise on a softball field and not everyone likes to socialize on a park bench.) Another difficulty involves communication. Recreational needs have to be described accurately so that they can be understood by other people—whether landscape architects, teachers, maintenance men, politicians, city planners, coaches, or neighbors and friends.

A common obstacle to understanding and communicating our recreational needs, and to realizing solutions to them, is our habit of asking for a specific product we have used or seen (even if it has been a failure) rather than analyzing our need and thinking about all the possible ways of meeting it. For example, we concern ourselves with beautiful light poles, when the issue is lighting; we concern ourselves with the number of policemen, when the issue is safety; we concern ourselves with signs, when the issue is being able to get around and knowing where we are; we concern ourselves with building playgrounds, when our real need is for recreational opportunities. And so what we have, too often, is a collection of *products* which don't solve the problems they were supposed to.

Karl Linn on Performance
The performance of small scale design solutions for urban areas can be evaluated on their ability to satisfy the needs of their users. Although the design space is often quite small, the complexities of that environment require that the product satisfy frequently conflicting needs of different sectors within the same community. The difficulty is compounded because these groups often cannot articulate their views. Karl Linn, in his Neighborhood Commons work in Philadelphia and Washington, found that the successful performance of a solution depended upon the design team's ability to understand the problem.

"A lot of people have moved into non-ownership tenancy, especially in the congested urban centers, where rental housing was available to those who could not afford ownership or preferred not to be burdened by it. An open public space in the city should function like a 'backyard' or a 'country club' by being jointly administered by the respective public agencies and by the residents. . . .

"We have to shift from the concept of passive spectator use of public open spaces to one that accommodates the emergence of an intensive urban style of living. . . .

"The agency personnel which introduced us to neighborhoods in Philadelphia and the social service agencies which co-sponsored the project in Washington, were unable to develop trust relationships with teenagers and young men. Even the civil rights organizations which we contacted at that time were more interested in protesting than in building. Consequently our work focused primarily on the needs of mothers. We ended up building a lot of sandboxes, but soapboxes were not on our list, and teenagers often vandalized the projects, since their interests had not been taken into consideration. A neighborhood park is neither an ordinary park scaled down, nor a tot lot. . . .

"Since a neighborhood is a place in which young and old, boys and girls converge, an open space within the block must provide for many uses. As we responded to the mothers' request to create playgrounds, not neighborhood forums, the interests of men were again ignored. . . .

"If black communities have any priority, it is the cultivation of male leadership, which socially aware designers should be able to facilitate through the development of the appropriate kind of space."
From "Neighborhood Commons" by Karl Linn, in *Architectural Design*, August 1968.

We would do a lot better if we asked who a particular solution was for, what it was for, and how it was supposed to work. Finding and evaluating the answers to these questions will tell us how a particular recreational facility *performs*—in other words, how it meets the needs of the people who use it. *Performance* is the measure of how well our environment responds to our needs, and the basis of a common vocabulary for communicating our needs to others.

The next part of this book describes the component factors of performance that must be considered in analyzing your recreational needs and determining the best solutions to them. Some of these component factors concern aspects of people and activities and their requirements. Others deal with aspects of spaces and what they permit or prohibit. Many of the component factors are described as continuums, because thorough consideration of them requires dealing with a wide range of examples between two extremes. One factor, linear/nonlinear, is treated as a comparison between two opposite kinds of spaces. And the rest are described as additional components of recreational spaces. Together, they provide a system for identifying and analyzing the performance requirements of your recreational needs and their solutions.

National Parks Performance
This year marks the one hundredth anniversary of the National Park System—which began with Yellowstone Park —a vast network of open public recreation land which has served as a prototypical park system for 102 other countries around the world.

But American parks are in trouble. Two hundred million tourists visit these recreation areas annually and, to cope with increases in people, the National Park Service has had to increase the existing service facilities many times. In Yellowstone alone, 2½ million visitors annually have required the addition of 2100 new buildings, 30 sewer systems, ten electric systems, 750 miles of road and 3000 campsites.

Bumper-to-bumper traffic, pollution, overcrowding, crime, and drugs have extended the problems of the city to our open space. One reaction to this impending disaster has come from the Conservation Foundation, which has called for a complete redefinition of the parks and their purpose.

National Parks for the Future, a 254-page report by conservation-minded citizens all over the U.S., suggests that a distinction be made between national park areas and "others"; the 172 historic areas, the 37 national recreation areas, and park locations near urban centers. These "other" areas should be removed from the jurisdiction of the National Park Service and operated by a separate federal bureau. The report stresses preservation. Its recommendations include:

Limiting autos in parks, because they "can destroy our national park heritage just as surely as they have desecrated much of our urban countryside."

Declaring a moratorium on roadbuilding in the parks.

Banning wheeled campers as "contrary to the park ethic."

Phasing motel, food, and recreation concessions out of the parks and relocating them outside park boundaries.

When President Theodore Roosevelt first saw the Grand Canyon in 1903 he said, "Leave it as it is. You cannot improve on it."

But parks are for people and there are certainly those who deserve to enjoy the open spaces and yet are unable to backpack several miles or sleep on the ground in a pup tent.

Yosemite Park has found a solution to problems of auto and campfire pollution, overcrowding, and drugs. Following directives from Washington, a new breed of rangers teach ecology courses and keep visiting kids and adults interested and involved. Double-decked buses, powered by nonpolluting propane fuel, have replaced the plague of private cars. Caravans and most cars must be left in specified lots.

George B. Hartzon, National Park Service director, defines the problem confronting the parks as one of attitude: "The real crunch coming in this country is to articulate an environmental ethic to guide corporate and human conduct —and this speaks basically to the issue that man is part of his environment. The practical problem is that we know how many elk a park can handle ecologically but not how many people."

The future use and developmental direction of our national parks is a crucial concern in the overall question of recreation: how do we most effectively bring urban man and unspoiled nature into symbiotic balance and still preserve the needs and integrity of both.

Inactive/Active

Perhaps the reason that so many of us think first of strenuous exercise when we think of recreation is that we probably spend most of our time indoors, and most of that time sitting down. But if we think for a minute about all the time when we are not involved in routine, and all the time we are not playing an active sport, we will see how much of our free time we choose to spend in ways that are physically not very active. It might be reading or picnicking in the shade of a tree; walking along a wooded path; floating on our back in the middle of a lake; or digging weeds in our garden.

Inactive

"All forms of recreation may, in the first place, be conveniently arranged under two general heads. One will include all of which the predominating influence is to stimulate exertion of any part or parts needing it; the other, all which cause us to receive pleasure without conscious exertion. Games chiefly of mental skill, as chess, or athletic sports, as baseball, are examples of means of recreation of the first class, which may be termed that of exertive recreation; music and the fine arts generally of the second or receptive division."
Public Parks and the Enlargement of Towns.

Nineteenth century outdoor public recreation was much less physically active than today's. It ranged from children's games like tug-of-war, to lawn tennis and ice skating, both of which were encouraged by Olmsted's parks.

Our recreational needs embrace the entire continuum of physical activity. Sports like handball and soccer, which have no rest periods in the course of an entire game, would be classified as among the most active. Bicycling and casual swimming could be called moderately active. You can see that the distinctions can be very fine.

Thinking about your recreational preferences in terms of this continuum, and placing each activity you like somewhere along it, will demonstrate the wide degree of activity that we like to include in our recreational life and underscore the importance of providing for it.

Active

Football

Football, in the form we know it today, stems from the "Boston game" as played at Harvard in the 1870's and patterned after rugby rules. In November 1876, a new Intercollegiate Football Association, which codified the rules of modern football, was founded at Springfield College. Football became a highly popular sport at eastern colleges and universities and became a professional sport in 1895. The National Football League was founded in Canton, Ohio, in 1920.

The original football was a Danish person's skull, in the eleventh century. Due to thin boot construction of the era and bruised toes, a leather ball filled with hair was adopted. This evolved into air-filled pig bladders and further elongated into the conventional football used today.

Field size is 300 by 160 feet plus end zones. Goal posts are 24 feet apart. The game is divided into four periods of 15 minutes each, with a one minute rest between periods and a 15-minute intermission after the first two periods.

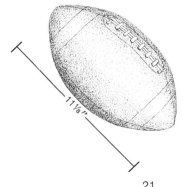

Individual/Group

Whether we prefer inactive or active forms of recreation, and whatever our age, we can enjoy recreation alone or as part of a group of almost any size. Although it's usual for us to think that the number of people involved in an activity is determined by specific game rules, there are actually three categories of activities which determine the number of people involved differently.

The first consists of spontaneous, free-form activities that are such an important part of our recreational experience, such as walks, picnics, and swimming at the beach. The number of people involved in these pursuits is completely flexible. In the second, mentioned above, the number of people is determined by game rules, whether the game is for an individual (solitaire), for two people (chess or tennis), or ten people (basketball). The third

Individual

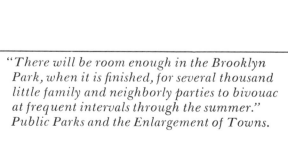

"There will be room enough in the Brooklyn Park, when it is finished, for several thousand little family and neighborly parties to bivouac at frequent intervals through the summer."
Public Parks and the Enlargement of Towns.

category is determined by the physical capacity of a facility: sports events with a limited number of seats or an outdoor concert which can only be heard within a certain radius of the bandshell, are examples.

All three categories include activities for one person, for a few people, and for larger groups of people—from a solitary walk to a family picnic to a spontaneous rally; from solitaire to ping-pong to a swimming meet; from a park bench to a merry-go-round to a stadium. Most people want to spend some time alone, some time with a close friend or among relatives, and some time as part of a large crowd. As a result, leisure pursuits, games, and facilities have evolved to accommodate the entire range of group size.

Group

Volleyball

Volleyball was invented at Springfield College in 1895 for the Holyoke YMCA. It has since spread to some 70 countries around the world. The rules are simple and have changed little since the game's inception. A team has six players (except in the Orient where there are nine) and equipment consists only of a net (or rope) and a ball. Volleyball has remained strictly an amateur sport and was admitted to the Olympic program in Tokyo in 1964.

The official court is 60 by 30 feet, divided in half by a net three feet wide suspended five feet above the ground. The ball is 26 to 27 inches in circumference, weighs nine to ten ounces and is inflated to seven to eight pounds of pressure. The object of the game is to hit the ball back and forth across the net, preventing it from touching the ground within the team's own court.

A game consists of eight minutes of playing time. It takes about 20 minutes to play a regular game.

"Consider that the New York Park and the Brooklyn Park are the only places in those associated cities where ... you will find a body of [people] coming together ... all classes largely represented ..., each individual adding by his mere presence to the pleasure of all others, all helping to the greater happiness of each. You may thus often see vast numbers of persons brought closely together, poor and rich, young and old.... I have seen a hundred thousand thus congregated."
Public Parks and the Enlargement of Towns.

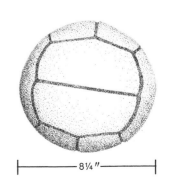

├─── 8¼″ ───┤

Young/Old

An infant rocking contently in a baby carriage; a two-year old with pail and shovel in a sandbox; a young child testing his muscles and coordination on a jungle-gym; an older child learning how to shoot baskets; an old couple sitting on a bench talking.

If you are past childhood and not yet restricted in your activities by old age, you may have forgotten how many choices and limitations of recreational experience are determined on the basis of age. Age is a factor encouraging or discouraging *interest*, and a major factor in defining physical *capability*. Young children are not interested in sitting quietly on

Frisbee

The frisbee was introduced in California in the early 1950's by an enterprising individual named Fred Morrison who used it as a county fair gimmick to prove the existence of (and sell) "invisible string."

Initially marketed in California under the name "Pluto Planets," both name and design were modified, from "Wham-O flying saucer" to "Frisbee," and the ridge pattern was patented.

Frisbee, now an international fad, comes in a variety of sizes, styles, and prices: Mini-Frisbee, Regular Frisbee, All-American Frisbee, Moonlighter Frisbee (which is phosphorescent), Master Frisbee, and the Fastback Frisbee that sacrifices distance for speed. In an effort to sound Continental, the manufacturer lists each frisbee's weight in grams (there are roughly 28½ grams to the ounce).

Recorded throwing techniques include backhand, underhand, and sidearm throws and curves, skip shots, and wrist and thumb flips. Documented games include catch, follow-the-leader, frisbee marathons, keepaway, and a team endurance tournament called "guts frisbee."

|— 9½″ —|

Young

"Young children, when confined to the city during the summer, generally suffer in health. . . . When it is impracticable to make a visit of some length to the country with them, great advantage will be gained by spending the greater part of a day . . . in the open air, and under conditions otherwise favorable to health."
To Those Having the Care of Young Children, handbill, 1872.

benches; infants cannot climb jungle-gyms; older children don't like to play in sandboxes; and older men and women don't have the stamina for basketball.

It is easy to forget, in thinking about the recreational profile of a neighborhood, how much people's age influences their need for particular recreational opportunities.

There are, however, many activities that are appropriate to several different age groups. Camping, for example, can be enjoyed by a two-year-old or a seventy-year-old and by almost anyone in between. A hike or bicycle ride appeals equally to the young person and the middle-aged.

Finally there are activities that can be enjoyed equally by all groups and in which they can participate together. Sunbathing, people-watching, picnics, sports events, outdoor plays and concerts, and outings are activities which can bring all the generations together.

Mixed age groups

Old

"Cultivate the habit of thoughtful attention to the feebler sort of folk—of asking, for instance, can this or that be made easier and more grateful to an old woman or a sick child, without, on the whole, additional expense, except in thoughtfulness? If so, ten to one, the little improvement will simply be that refinement of judgment which is the larger part of the difference between good and poor art, and the enjoyment of every man will be increased by it, though he may not know just how."
Mount Royal.

Shuffleboard

Shuffleboard, a derivative of lawn bowling, began in England around the thirteenth century. The earliest record of the game in New England was its denunciation as a gambler's sport, and it was outlawed in certain areas in 1845. The game appears to have picked up again in the 1870's when it became a chief feature of entertainment for passengers on the ocean liner voyage between England and Australia.

It was reintroduced in Florida after World War II and by 1951 it was estimated that there were about 5000 public courts in 455 cities. It is played by all ages, although it is especially popular among older people.

The court is 52 by 6 feet with a concrete or terrazzo surface. The composition disks are one inch thick, six inches in diameter, and weigh between 11½ and 15 ounces. The strategy of the game is to knock a rival's disk out of position in a scoring box, replacing it with your own. Each player or team shoots eight disks each round.

|← 6″ →|

Specific/Nonspecific

What can you do on a slide? Slide. What can you do on a bicycle path? Ride a bicycle, walk, or jog. What can you do in a big grassy meadow? Walk, run, jump, play catch, tag or stickball, fly a kite, ride a horse, picnic, chase a butterfly, sleep. The list could go on and on, because the meadow does not have restrictions of size, shape, or equipment.

Some spaces, either by accident or design, will permit only one specific activity to take place. A space may be too small for anything but checkers or one park bench, too narrow for anything except walking or bicycle riding, or too hilly and rocky for anything but climbing. It may be covered by a basketball court, or by some other specific and limiting solution to a particular recreational need.

There are also spaces that can be used for a few similar activities, either simultaneously or sequentially. These spaces have a moderate degree of specificity. Croquet, bocce, horseshoes, and badminton could all be played on the same,

Badminton
Badminton is considered one of the fastest of the court games. It originated in India centuries ago under the name of Poona and was introduced to England in the 1860's by British Army officers. It had no name until 1873 when the Duke of Beaufort introduced it at a party at his country place, "Badminton." The name was adopted and its rules standardized in 1887. Badminton became popular in this country in 1929 and is now played in international competition (the Thomas Cup) in three zones: American, European and Pacific. The shuttlecock (called a "birdie" or shuttle) has a semi-spherical cork head 1 to 1⅛ inches in diameter and contains 14 to 16 feathers, each 2½ inches long, imbedded in the flat cork face and rising like a crown with a 2½ inch spread at the top. The shuttlecock weighs between ⅙ and ⅕ of an ounce.

Specific

Moderately specific

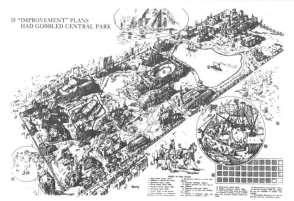

├ 1 to 1⅛ʺ ┤

"The first condition of a good park, therefore, is that from the start a limited number of leading ends shall be fixed upon to serve which as well as possible will compel opportunity for serving others on the space allotted to it to be excluded."
Notes on the Plan of Franklin Park and Related Matters.

IF "IMPROVEMENT" PLANS HAD GOBBLED CENTRAL PARK

Central Park was designed by Olmsted specifically to cultivate the illusion of a rambling rural countryside in the midst of a city. But generations of well-intentioned New Yorkers have seen Central Park's *open* spaces as *empty* spaces. By now the park could easily have been filled many times with buildings proposed in the name of improvement. This cartoon, published in *The New York Times* in 1918, describes schemes ranging from a huge outdoor theater and a graveyard to a merchandise exhibition structure and a site for trenches supposedly essential to the Liberty Loan campaign.

reasonably small, flat space. A lake is another example: limited to water activities and further controlled by seasonal, weather, and temperature conditions, it still permits a range of different activities to take place at the same time.

Finally, there are spaces which are so generous in size or so general in what they provide—like the meadow—that they allow a great range of activities.

You might conclude, then, that it would be simple and economical to provide nothing but big, unspecific recreational space. But this is not always possible, and not a good idea where there is a genuine need for recreational experiences that can be met only by specific—even though inflexible—solutions.

Nonspecific

Below are pictured two spaces, an activity, and an object. For the spaces, write in all the different things you could do there. For the activity, write in the different spaces where it could take place. And for the rubber ball, write some of the many games you could play with it. You will see that the specificity of spaces, activities, and equipment greatly affect our recreational opportunities.

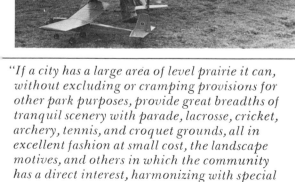

"If a city has a large area of level prairie it can, without excluding or cramping provisions for other park purposes, provide great breadths of tranquil scenery with parade, lacrosse, cricket, archery, tennis, and croquet grounds, all in excellent fashion at small cost, the landscape motives, and others in which the community has a direct interest, harmonizing with special motives of recreation of particular classes."
Mount Royal.

Rubber ball

Small/Large

We're all familiar with the size of many recreational spaces, from a vest-pocket park or playground to a national forest; and with the size requirements of specific activities, from checkers to football. However, there are many available spaces that don't fit neatly into ordinary size classifications, and many free-form activities that have real, but not specifically defined, space needs.

How much space does a picnic take? Surely, you could set up a grill and blanket in close quarters; but much of the enjoyment in picnicking comes from a sense of space and the refreshing environment of woods or stream. How much space do you need to feel alone? How long a path do you need for a walk to be really enjoyable?

Chess

Chess dates back at least 6000 years; the Greeks, Romans, Babylonians, Arabs, Hindus, Castilians, Irish, Mesopotamians, Welsh, Hebrews, Chinese, Scythians, and Araucanians have all been credited with beginning it.

The Chinese Mandarin Han Sing (born in 174 B.C.) supposedly devised the game to keep his soldiers entertained during the idle winter months. Called *Choke-Choo-Hong-Ki,* meaning "science of wars," historians point out the similarity between chess moves and military strategy. In 1930, a crude chess board, chess men, and markers were discovered in the tomb of King Tut-Ankh-Amen of Egypt who died more than 1200 years before the birth of the Chinese Mandarin.

The first written statement and game rules were developed in 1200 A.D. in Italy with the first international tournament played in 1562 between Italy and Spain. Play has continued on both national and international levels, and world champions have been generally recognized since 1843. The world team championships, instituted in 1927, have been won most often by Russia. The Fischer-Spassky match in Reykjavik in 1972, considered to be the most important in the game's history, was the first world chess championship to be played outside Moscow since 1948.

Small

"It follows that so far as any purpose of public grounds can be well provided for on a small ground, it is better to so provide for it, rather than to multiply and complicate the purposes to be provided for on a larger ground." Notes on the Plan of Franklin Park and Related Matters.

Such a small park is Tompkins Park (whose site is now occupied by a building) in Brooklyn, designed as a place for neighborhood people to sit.

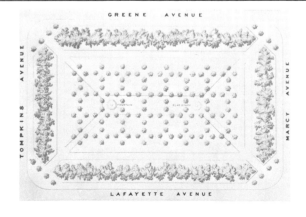

"Spaciousness is of the essence of a park.... There are countless things to be desired for the people of a city, an important element of the cost of providing which is ground space. It is the consequent crowded condition of a city that makes the sight of merely uncrowded ground in a park the relief and refreshment to the mind that it is." Notes on the Plan of Franklin Park and Related Matters.

Size is a response not just to the number of people involved in an activity, but to the nature of the activity as well. Some activities are best served by efficient, compact areas, while others suggest rambling, undefined spaces. Some activities can take place adjacent to any other, but others need space around them for quiet, for safety, or for spectators. Size is one of the elements to be used to enhance a recreational experience, and understanding the needs that can be met by a space of a certain size is one of the most important aspects of utilizing space for recreation.

Large

"The establishment by government of great public grounds for the free enjoyment of the people . . . is . . . justified and enforced as a political duty."
The Yosemite Valley and the Mariposa Big Trees, a Preliminary Report, 1865.

At left, the Vale of Kashmir in Prospect Park. At right, an illustration of the Mariposa Big Tree Grove about 1863.

Golf
The earliest mention of golf occurs in a prohibiting law passed by the Scottish Parliament in March 1457, under which "golfe be utterly cryed downe." Its development thereafter was hindered by various royal decrees which continued to ban the game until 1545, when it was first played openly by Mary Queen of Scots. The first official tournament, which became the British Open, was played in 1869. There is no clear record of when golf was introduced to this country.

The earliest golf balls were made of feathers tightly stuffed into thin leather bags. The liveliness of the ball depended on how well it had been stuffed. Later, a ball made of gutta percha, a sticky resin substance, was designed, still with a limited driving range. In 1899 an American named Haskell invented the rubber core ball which was adopted for official use in 1902.

The present official ball in the U.S. weighs 1.62 ounces and is 1.68 inches in diameter. A round of golf is 18 holes (holes range in length from 100 to 600 yards).

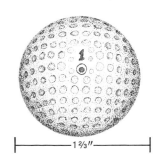

├─── 1 ⅔" ───┤

Linear/Nonlinear

You're probably pretty confident that you know the size of a football field, especially if you play the game or watch it on television. You're used to measuring it in your mind by the kind of activity that takes place on it, and by seeing all of it used at once. But did you know that if the area of a football field were a bicycle path five feet wide, it could wind along a river, cut through a wood, or parallel a street for over two miles!

This example demonstrates that the shape of recreational space is just as important as its size. Just as there are activities that have to take place in defined *areas*—rectangles, squares, or circles—there are other activities that are *linear* in nature, such as walking, bicycling, horseback riding, and canoeing. While it's true that you could take a walk across a football field or canoe across

Bicycling
The first two-wheeled bicycle was designed in Paris in 1690 by M. de Sivrac but proved rather unsatisfactory because it lacked pedals. Other efforts followed but it wasn't until 1821 that Louis Gompertz of England invented a gear-type rope system which became the basic bicycle chain.

Experiments continued with wheel size changes: large in front, small in back, and vice-versa. The "high wheeler" evolved, made only of wood except for the tires, which were covered with iron. In 1868 hard rubber tires replaced the wooden and iron ones; spokes of wire instead of wood were added in 1869.

In 1885, the English designed a bike whose front wheel wasn't much bigger than its back which made easier riding and exceptional speed possible. In 1888 J. B. Dunlop invented the pneumatic tire, which revolutionized pleasure bicycling and introduced it as a racing sport. His basic tire structure, an outside rubber cover supported by an air-filled inner tube, is still the standard today.

|— 26 or 27″ —|

Nonlinear

The strip picture at the right is a slice of New York City's Central Park, seen from above, with south at the left, north at the right. It is a combination of an engraving of the park in 1870 and a recent aerial photograph. The major change that can be seen is the replacement of the Old Reservoir by ballfields. Some of the changes that cannot be seen are: an addition of 27 acres of space for buildings, services, and parking between 1900 and 1966; a tripling of paved walks and drives in the same

time; the enclosure of 30 acres for special activities; and the reduction of open meadow between 1900 and 1966 from 55 to 16 acres. The area of city north of the park is included to demonstrate that linear and nonlinear spaces are a characteristic of nearly every environment.

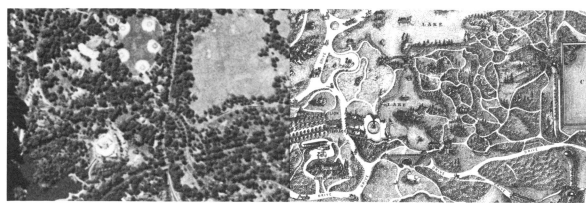

Linear

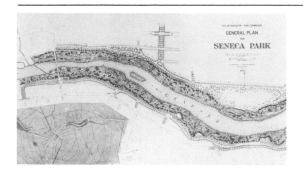

Linear parks were a favorite with Olmsted. Like Seneca Park in Rochester, they were often suggested by a topographical feature, in this case the Genesee River. As a result of such a shape, these linear parks preserved the natural beauty of the river scenery and its water for recreational uses, kept natural drainage systems intact, cut down water pollution by using the river for non-industrial purposes, and held the main surface water channels in public control.

a lake, neither of these activities is as well suited to those sites as to a long, winding space.

Knowing the potential of variously shaped areas can help you maximize their recreational possibilities. And knowing the shape requirements and alternatives of different recreational activities makes it easier for you to understand the potential of recreational spaces. Nonlinear spaces are often created by the intersection or deviation of linear systems, and usually surrounded, bisected, or connected by them as well.

The photographs below, from ground level and from above, show some of the huge variety of linear and nonlinear spaces, and how they fit together. If we learn to open our eyes to all the funny-shaped, left-over spaces around us—especially places like streets, sidewalks, vacant lots and rooftops—we might find solutions to a lot of our recreational needs near at hand.

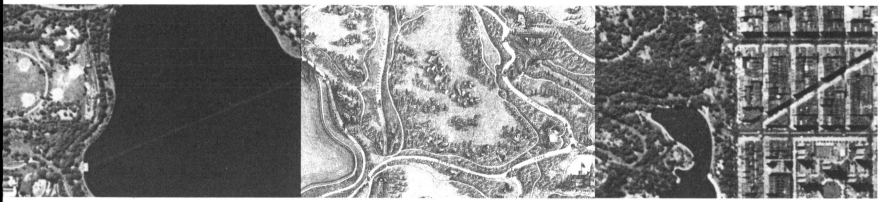

Baseball

Baseball, the American derivative of the English games of cricket and rounders, was first developed in this country around 1800. Haphazard versions of the so-called "Town Ball Game" grew up in Boston, New York, and Philadelphia between 1820 and 1833. The rules were standardized in 1842 and the first baseball organization, the New York City-based Knickerbocker Baseball Club, was formed in 1845. The earliest game on record under the standardized rules was on 19 June 1846 in Hoboken, New Jersey. In 1871, the first professional baseball association, known as the National Association of Professional Baseball Players, was organized.

The playing field consists of the infield, a diamond 90 feet square, and the outfield, with a 300-foot hitting distance. The official baseball has a cork and rubber core, wound with yarn, and covered in stitched-on leather. The ball must not weigh less than five ounces nor more than 5¼ ounces, and must be between nine and 9¼ inches in circumference.

2⅞"

31

Flat/Sloped

Cliffs, mountains, valleys, and rolling hills aren't just good to look at; they're good to use. If you live in a city (other than San Francisco and other hilly cities) and don't get much of a chance to wander over topographically interesting terrain, or if you strongly prefer games played on prepared flat surfaces, recreation to you is flat. But there are a great many interesting activities that can only be pursued on terrain that slopes: skiing, sledding, and rolling down a hill, for example. There are also activities that can take place on several different kinds of topography, but which are made more enjoyable by stretching across a hill or two, such as hiking and golf.

The drawing below represents different topographies from absolutely vertical to absolutely horizontal, both above and below ground. Above the drawing is a list of different activities. Draw a line from each activity that needs a specific kind of topography to the appropriate terrain in the drawing. Then, in the column provided at the right, write in the activities that can take place on a variety of topographies.

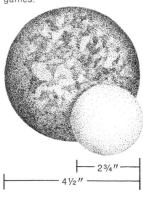

2¾"
4½"

Lawn bowling · Back-packing · Making an echo · Catching a fish · Writing poetry · Playing baseball · Scaling a cliff · Picnicking · Surfing · King of the Mountain · Sailing · Exploring a cave · Building a sand castle · Skiing · Playing hide-and-seek · Playing croquet · Golfing · Skipping rocks · Rolling down a hill · Walking a dog · Sledding · Playing shuffleboard · Camping out · Skindiving · Throwing a frisbee · Playing tag · Riding a horse · Sightseeing · Finding seashells · Climbing a mountain · Painting a picture · Sleeping in the grass · Playing tennis · Daydreaming · Hiking · Bicycling

"It is a mistake to suppose that a considerable extent of nearly flat ground is inadmissible or undesireable in a great park, or that it must be overcome, at any cost, by vast artificial elevations and depressions, or by covering all the surface with trivial objects of interest." Chicago South Park Report, 1871.

At right, profiles of Central Park south-to-north along Sixth and Seventh Avenues.

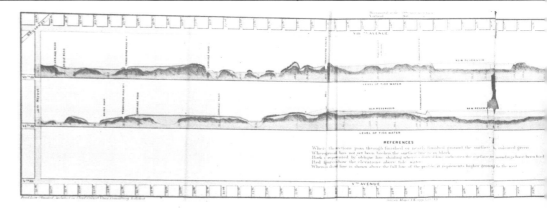

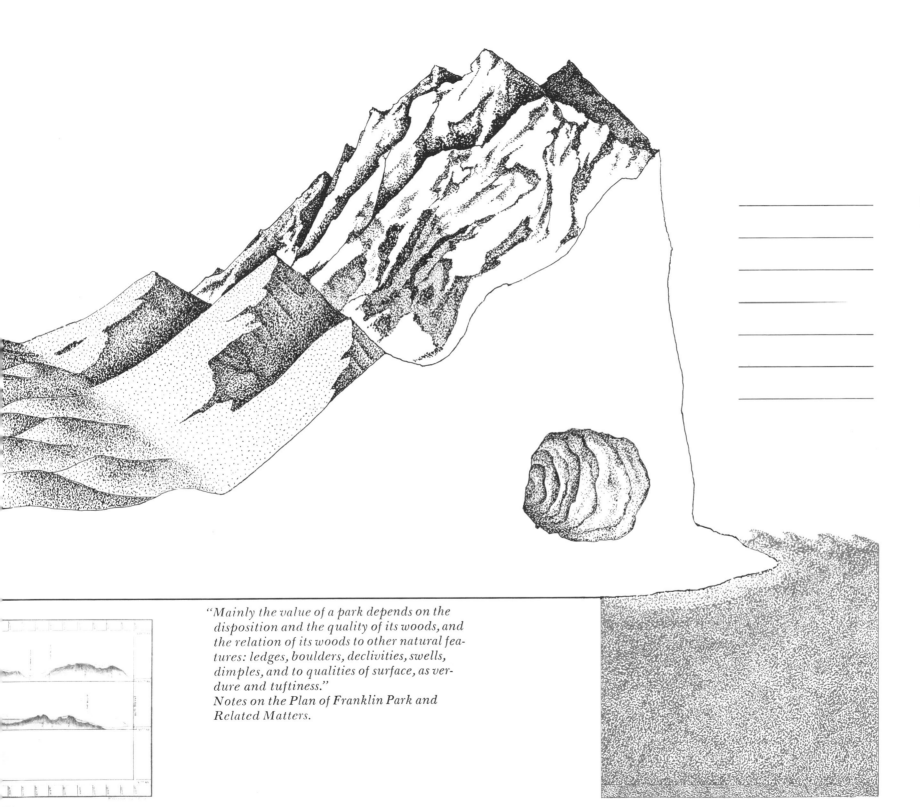

"*Mainly the value of a park depends on the disposition and the quality of its woods, and the relation of its woods to other natural features: ledges, boulders, declivities, swells, dimples, and to qualities of surface, as verdure and tuftiness.*"
Notes on the Plan of Franklin Park and Related Matters.

Skiing
The earliest ski edges were bones from large animals, strapped to the skis with leather thongs. The oldest pair of skis (purportedly 5000 years old) was found in Sweden.

Skis were first used in warfare in the Battle of Oslo in 1200 A.D. and proved so effective they became standard army equipment by the 1500's.

The bone ski had no standard size and was not turned up at the ends. Centuries later, when wood was substituted, the standard size became 7'6" long, about 2" thick, and 5" wide with about one foot of the front end of the ski turned up.

Skiing was introduced into Central Europe via Austria in 1590. It is not known how skis originated in North America, whether they were fashioned by native Indians or evolved out of the Canadian snowshoes. However, during the rush to the Pacific coast for gold in the 1850's, skis were in evidence in the Sierra Nevadas and in 1840 it was stated that "wooden blades, for use on ice and snow," were brought from Norway and were used by the immigrants along the north Atlantic coast.

Access and Distribution

How many and what kind of people will be served by a recreational facility depends not only on its size and type but on its location as well. You are probably familiar with areas or neighborhoods that don't have nearly enough recreational spaces or in which the spaces they do have are unsuitable; and areas that seem to have more recreational space than is being used. These situations may be the result of bad planning originally, or of a shortage of available funds. Very often such disparities are the result of the fact that the available recreational facilities are unable to keep up with changing neighborhood needs and recreational patterns.

Over the years, categories of recreational spaces have been developed to combine flexibility with long-term value: the tot-lot

In Boston, Olmsted planned an "emerald necklace" of green spaces fulfilling a variety of purposes, from the rural landscape of Franklin Park through the forest of the Arnold Arboretum to the drainage control system of the Fens. This urban park *system* became the basis for a metropolitan network of open spaces developed later by Charles Eliot. Similarly, Olmsted's work in other cities provided a structure for linking and expanding open spaces on urban, regional, and even national levels. At left, an Olmsted plan for Boston; at right, a diagram of the Boston park system in 1899.

or vest-pocket park designed to serve a block or two; the neighborhood park or playfield designed to serve a small homogeneous area and intended to be convenient to all; the city park designed to serve a small city or one of several areas of a large metropolis; and the national park or regional wilderness, intended to preserve spectacles of nature in a way that will accommodate all who wish to see them.

As we consider how many and what kind of people each of these facilities can serve, we can also ask: how many tot-lots does one block need; how many playfields are appropriate for one neighborhood; how many large parks would one large city use; and how great an area of national park does one state or region require? By answering these questions in general and in specific instances we can decide whether an area can best be

served by concentrated or dispersed facilities, and how recreational space can best be distributed in order to be effective for the greatest number of people.

At left, superimposed over the base map of Boston, are shown the residential population density (black circles) and the public park space (green squares).
From *Urban Atlas: Twenty American Cities*, by Joseph R. Passonneau and Richard Saul Wurman.

At right, America's increasing urbanization is shown relative to the location of federally-held public land, including: national parks, monuments, seashores, and recreation areas; national wildlife refuges; and national forests and purchase units. The population indications are exact; the public open land areas are approximate.
From *The National Atlas*.

The Urban Explosion
In 1860, while Central Park was being constructed, America's population (a bit over 30,000,000) was 80% rural and only 20% urban. Today, 110 years later, those percentages are reversed while the population has nearly septupled. Of our present population of more than 200,000,000, fully 75% of us live in urban areas. That makes our *urban population 25 times as large* today as in 1860.

In addition, the 75% of our population living in urban areas have only 9% of our public recreational land. Ninety-one per cent of our public recreational land (the great majority of which is federally-owned) is located in non-urban areas of the country.

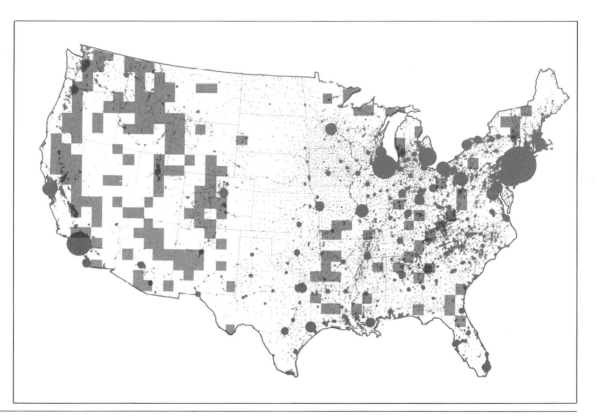

Distribution
"Many cities have moved strongly into the use of mobile recreation units which are able to bring specialized recreation activities into different neighborhoods quickly, and with a minimum of cost and capital investment. Such portable and mobile units are much less expensive than building a network of comparable facilities throughout the city would be. By rotating units, with specially trained leaders, from location to location and remaining at each one only while interest is at its height, it is possible to provide great variety and enrichment in disadvantaged neighborhoods and middle- and upper-class areas as well."
Community Council of Greater New York and the New York Foundation, *Urban Parks and Recreation: Challenge of the 1970's*, 1972.

Los Angeles operates 300 separate facilities on 217 sites. These include 144 well-equipped large recreation centers, 71 large parks, 50 swimming pools, ten Senior Citizens Centers, 13 golf courses, 14 miles of public beaches, 226 tennis courts, 73 miles of bridle trails, 81 miles of hiking trails, 15 museums and cultural centers, 62 shuffle-board courts, seven archery ranges, seven historical sites, and seven park lakes. In addition, the Los Angeles park and recreation department operates numerous other specialized facilities

"If recreations requiring large spaces to be given up to the use of a comparatively small number are not considered essential, numerous small grounds so distributed through a large town that some one of them could be easily reached by a short walk from every house, would be more desirable than a single area of great extent, however rich in landscape attractions it might be. Especially would this be the case if the numerous local grounds were connected and supplemented by a series of trunk-roads or boulevards."
Public Parks and the Enlargement of Towns.

"A site for a park to stand by itself and be little used except by those living near it should be a very different one from that for a park designed for more general use, and especially for a park which is to stand as one of a series. In the latter case the fitness of a site will largely be found in its adaptation to supply some form of park refreshment that others of the series are ill-adapted to supply or are naturally excluded from supplying."
Seventh Annual Report of the Board of Commissioners of the Department of Parks for the City of Boston for the Year 1881.

Movement

When you consider not only recreational activities themselves but also the necessity of getting in, out, and around recreational spaces, you can see that many different modes of movement have to be considered. There are walking, bicycling, horseback riding, and, of course, the automobile—all can provide a source of recreation as well as the access to it. In larger recreational areas service and maintenance vehicles must be considered, too.

Some movement modes are compatible and can share the same movement system at virtually all times, such as private cars and service vehicles. Other movement modes are incompatible to varying degrees: pedestrians and cars should never share the same movement system; bicycles and cars might, but ideally not at the same time.

"*Each of the transverse roads is intended to be sunk so far below the general surface that the park drives may, at every necessary point of intersection, be carried entirely over it, . . . and a little judicious planting on the tops or slopes of the banks above these walls will, in most cases, entirely conceal both the roads and the vehicles moving in them, from the view of those walking or driving in the park.*"
Description of a Plan for the Improvement of the Central Park, "Greensward," 1858.

"*A system of independent ways: 1st, for carriages; 2d, for horsemen wishing to gallop; 3d, for footmen; and 4th, for common street traffic requiring to cross the Park. By this means it was made possible, even for the most timid and nervous to go on foot to any district of the Park designed to be visited, without crossing a line of wheels on the same level, and consequently, without occasion for anxiety or hesitation. . . .*
"*To the visitor, carried by occasional defiles in the movement system from one field of landscape to another, in which a wholly dif-*"

In any case, movement patterns should not be allowed to just happen. Thought should be given to means of separating movement modes, such as time restrictions, curbs, fences, overpasses and underpasses, and grade and surface variations. Provisions should also be made for storage and resting places related to movement systems, such as benches, picnic tables, bicycle racks, snack bars, stables, parking lots, and service areas.

And consideration should be given to the possible negative influences an inappropriate movement system could have on the recreational area it was intended to serve.

Olmsted's scheme for the separation of movement systems in Central Park is justly renowned. When bicycles became popular, he made plans for their integration into the system. Below is a slice of the park, exaggerated in scale from west to east (top to bottom), showing the different corridors for pedestrians, bicycles, horses, in-park vehicles, and cross-park traffic, as well as the tree cover.

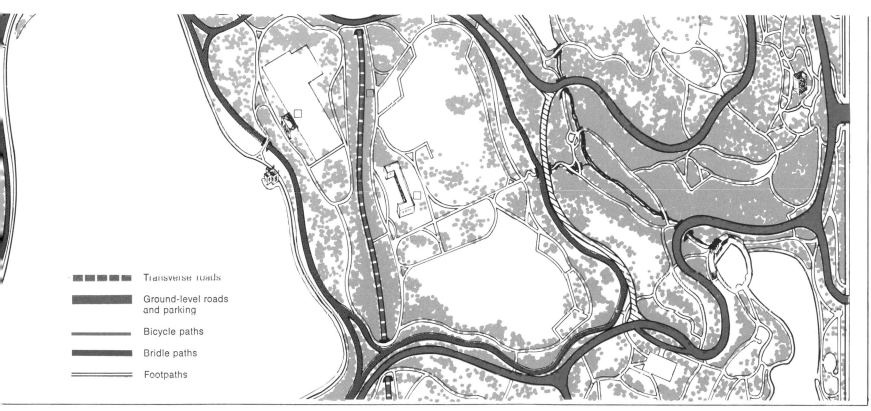

▬▬▬▬	Transverse roads
▬▬▬▬	Ground-level roads and parking
————	Bicycle paths
▬▬▬▬	Bridle paths
════	Footpaths

ferent series of details is presented, the extent of the Park is practically much greater than it would otherwise be."
Examination of the Design of the Park and of Recent Changes Therein, 1872.

At far left, a Central Park transverse road. At left, grade separation of roads and paths around the old reservoir in Central Park. At right, a rustic bridge for the carriage drive.

Future Movement Systems
Transportation systems of the future will provide a comprehensive movement network throughout the central city, urban recreational areas, and outlying regions. Examples of design solutions currently under consideration include the following.
Westinghouse Sky Bus
Electrically driven, highly automated bus-trains propelled along elevated roadways.
Tracked air cushion vehicle
A train which is suspended on a film of air. It is propelled forward on a single, central metal rail by a magnetic force. This power system is called a linear induction motor.
Bi-modal bus
A bus with special steel wheels, which can also be operated on railroad tracks.
Single-mode small car system
Small cars with automated controls and linear induction motors. They are dispatched at the patron's command over fixed routes.
Bi-modal small car system
Individual small battery-operated cars which can operate on city streets or on special electrified tracks.
Tube flight
Underground trains in tubes. Each vehicle floats on a cushion of compressed air and is propelled forward by pressurized air released from smaller tubes running parallel with the tube bed.

Safety and Comfort

So far we have talked mostly about providing space for recreational activities and about fulfilling the needs of people for specific recreational activities. Now let's talk for a moment about the quality of life in a recreational facility. On any occasion where we have a choice, we will choose an activity, a place, or a facility that offers us the amenities we need. Safety and comfort are two very important considerations.

People need to be protected from themselves, from other people, in some cases from animals, from traffic, and from dangerous features of the land. This can be done by a whole range of devices, both natural and artificial. Good lighting, careful supervision, and—most important—the presence of other people, can help make a park, or a street, safe during the day and night. Different kinds of traffic can be separated by curbs or fences. Signs can

Safety

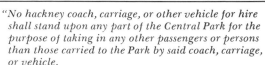

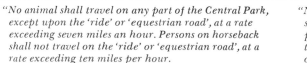

"No animal shall travel on any part of the Central Park, except upon the 'ride' or 'equestrian road', at a rate exceeding seven miles an hour. Persons on horseback shall not travel on the 'ride' or 'equestrian road', at a rate exceeding ten miles per hour.
"No vehicle shall be permitted on the 'ride' or 'equestrian road', the same being devoted exclusively to equestrians; nor shall any vehicle, horse, or animal of burden, go upon any part of the Central Park, except upon the 'drive', and other carriage and transverse roads, and upon such places as are appropriated for carriages at rest.
"No animal or vehicle shall be permitted to stand upon the 'drive', or carriage-roads, of Central Park, or any part thereof, to the obstruction of the way, or to the inconvenience of travel, nor shall any person upon the Central Park solicit or invite passengers.

"No hackney coach, carriage, or other vehicle for hire shall stand upon any part of the Central Park for the purpose of taking in any other passengers or persons than those carried to the Park by said coach, carriage, or vehicle.
"No omnibus, or express wagon, truck, or other vehicle carrying goods, merchandise, manure, soil, or other article shall be allowed to enter any part of Central Park, except upon the transverse roads."
Olmsted's Central Park regulations.

be used to note marshy ground or deep lakes, and railings can keep people away from sheer drops. Bushes can cushion falls, and soft ground and mats can protect high-jumpers and children on climbing-bars.

How much less satisfying recreation would be without comforts, even very simple ones. A roof of branches over a bicycle path to keep off the rain; a sunshade over park benches; bushes or trees to screen noise and unpleasant views; drinking fountains next to playing fields; restaurants and mobile hot dog stands at convenient intervals; and ramps as an

alternative to stairs for baby carriages, strollers, wagons, wheelchairs, and bicycles.

Comfort

What Trees Can Do for You
Trees help supply oxygen we need to breathe. Each acre of young trees can produce enough oxygen to keep 18 people alive. Trees help keep our air supply fresh by using up carbon dioxide that we exhale and that factories and engines emit.

Leaf surfaces trap and filter out ash, dust, and pollen particles carried in the air. Trees dilute gaseous pollutants in the air as they release oxygen.

Trees lower air temperature by using the sun's energy to evaporate water stored in their leaves. They increase humidity in dry climates by releasing moisture as a by-product of food-making and evaporation.

Trees cut noise pollution by acting as barriers to sound. Each 100-foot width of trees can absorb about six to eight decibels of sound intensity. Along busy highways, where traffic generates as much as 72 decibels, this noise reduction is welcome to residents of the area.

Trees break the onslaught of pelting raindrops on the soil surface and give the soil a chance to soak up as much water as possible. Tree leaves, when fallen, cover the ground to keep the soil from drying out. Tree roots help control soil erosion and keep silt out of streams and rivers.

"As commerce drives the people northward for their homes and means of communication are improved, if this number [of people using the park] should not often be several times multiplied, it can only be because the attractions of the park are counterweighted by the dangers, discomforts and annoyances which will arise from its crowded condition."
Letter to William Robinson, 1872.

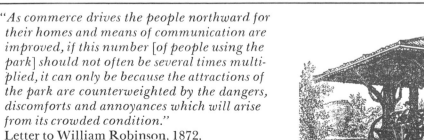

"Central Park . . . [has been] . . . furnished with a great variety of appliances, each . . . designed to be used in a different way and for different ends, though all for the one general end of the comfort of the occupants."
Instructions to the Keepers of Central Park, 1873.

Time,
Temperature,
Weather

When we imagine ourselves doing any one of the things we most like to do, the time, temperature, and weather are always just right for doing it. If we like to swim, we don't think of ourselves swimming outdoors in freezing weather; if we like to play tennis, we don't imagine ourselves playing on muddy courts in the pouring rain. But most of us live in areas with distinct seasonal changes. We can't swim outdoors in the cold, and when it rains outdoor tennis courts get wet.

An outdoor space is there twenty-four hours a day; it endures all temperatures and every kind of weather. But it will not be used under all these conditions. There are some activities that can be enjoyed only at certain times, in certain temperatures, and during certain kinds of weather. We have to consider, then, how time,

Temperature
The activities that you most enjoy are always related to the climate of where you live. Below is the average temperature in each season for six representative cities.

	Spring	Summer	Autumn	Winter
Boston	48	75	57	30
Miami	75	81	78	68
Duluth	30	68	40	10
Dodge City	50	80	57	30
Houston	68	84	75	55
San Francisco	55	58	60	50

On an average winter day, then, it will be almost 40° warmer in Miami than Boston or Dodge City, and almost 60° warmer in Miami than in Duluth. San Francisco, because it has such a consistently temperate climate, will be warmer than Boston or Duluth three-quarters of the year but cooler than either during the summer. You can see from the chart that Miami and Houston's recreational needs are heavily oriented toward summer-weather activities, that Duluth would logically lean toward cool-weather activities, and that Boston and Dodge City would be able to offer a wide range of activities by temperature depending on the availability of other natural factors, such as precipitation and terrain.

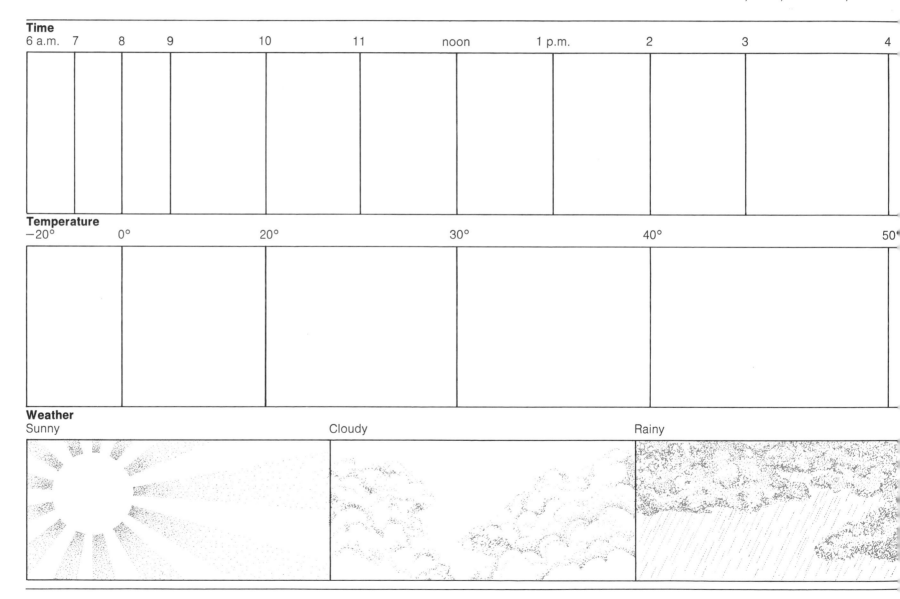

Time

6 a.m. | 7 | 8 | 9 | 10 | 11 | noon | 1 p.m. | 2 | 3 | 4

Temperature

−20° | 0° | 20° | 30° | 40° | 50°

Weather

Sunny | Cloudy | Rainy

temperature, and weather will encourage or restrict the full use and enjoyment of each recreational space.

Man has ways, of course, of modifying or even eliminating the restraints of time, temperature, and weather. Lighting, heating, and enclosed structures are among them. Sometimes these ways of making all things possible at all times are compatible with the larger goals and performances of outdoor public recreation, sometimes not. It is for you to decide which is more important in each case: the continuous availability of an activity; or retaining the natural appearance of the environment.

Below are three charts, divided into hour boxes, temperature zones, and weather conditions. In each zone, write in some of the activities that you can think of that could take place at that time, in that temperature, or during that kind of weather. Filling in the 3 p.m. box, the 70° box, and the sunny box will be easy, of course; some of the others will require more ingenuity.

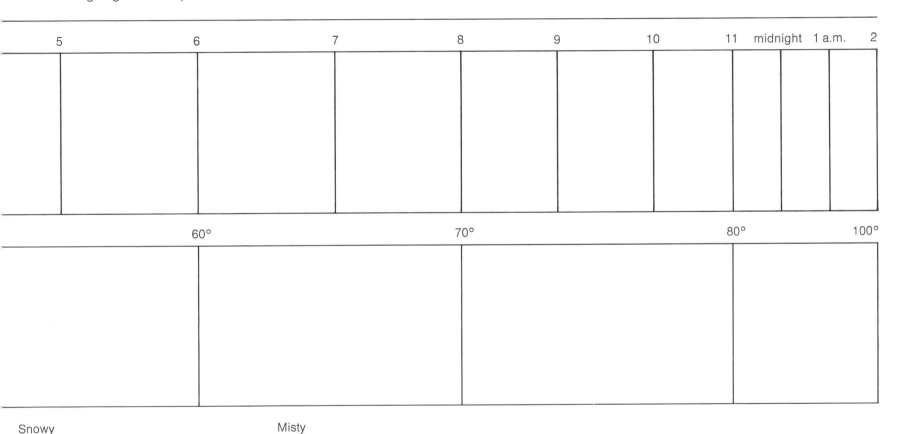

Precipitation
Annual precipitation:

Boston	32-48 inches
Miami	48-64 inches
Duluth	24-32 inches
Dodge City	16-24 inches
Houston	32-48 inches
San Francisco	8-16 inches

Number of days with at least one inch of snowfall in an average year:

Boston	10-20 days
Miami	0-8 days
Duluth	32-64 days
Dodge City	5-10 days
Houston	0-5 days
San Francisco	0-5 days

Mean annual snowfall:

Boston	32-64 inches
Miami	0-8 inches
Duluth	32-64 inches
Dodge City	16-32 inches
Houston	0-8 inches
San Francisco	0-0 inches

Later on in the book, when you're planning recreational areas, you can come back to these pages and see whether your plans are efficient in terms of their use during different times of day, at different temperatures, and in different seasons. The restrictions of time, temperature, and weather will challenge your use of recreational resources.

Preservation and Construction

Recreational spaces may be utilized essentially as they are found; or they may be constructed to fill specific recreational needs. It's important to realize, though, that whether a recreational space appears "natural"—with trees, grass, and streams—or "man-made"—perhaps a macadam playfield with steel structures—has very little to do with whether it was preserved or built.

In fact, there are virtually no recreational spaces that are truly "natural," which haven't been touched in some way by man's occupation of the planet. Even at the scale of our national forests, man-made programs and devices are crucial to their survival as we experience them: forests are thinned, dams built, and the animal population kept in balance. Central Park, which embodies the concept of providing the city-dweller with the oppor-

Central Park Construction
The bulk of construction on Central Park occurred between 1857 and 1861. During that time 500 acres out of the total 843 were drained and an extensive underground water run-off system was built. Four hundred acres were redug, topsoil added, and the subsoil mixed with fertilizing materials. Olmsted determined that, of the rest, 100 acres would be used for roads, ponds, and building sites, 50 acres would be rock and 150 acres reserved for the reservoirs.

Preservation

A machine for moving trees, used in the construction of Prospect Park in Brooklyn.

"What artist so noble ... as he who, with far-reaching conception of beauty and designing power, sketches the outlines, writes the colors, and directs the shadows of a picture so great that nature shall be employed upon it for generations, before the work he has arranged for her shall realize his intentions."
Walks and Talks of an American Farmer in England, 1852.

tunity to enjoy a "natural," rural environment, is in fact a man-made object. Marshes were drained, trees and bushes planted, hills and valleys sculpted, lakes and streams dug, and meadows seeded.

The land still left in a form approximating its truly natural state would be of little recreational use to us except in limited ways. Our ideas and ideals of nature are created to parallel our culture's standards of beauty and our needs. Nature's most important function in recreation is the aspects of performance it provides: beauty, refreshment, serenity. The nature of recreation is a vitally important—but not the only important—component factor in recreation, for we need playgrounds, swings, and tennis courts just as we need woods and grass and natural surroundings. So, whether a space is preserved or constructed is of little consequence; and whether it looks natural or man-made is only one of several aspects of how well we use, select, modify, and even create open space to meet our recreational needs.

Construction

"Why is it more irrational to . . . sympathetically cooperate with nature for the end which you have in view in your use of this property, than for that of raising apples, corn, or buckwheat, where nature left to herself, would not provide them?"
Mount Royal.

The photograph at far left shows an area of what was to become Central Park; the drawing at left is what Olmsted and Vaux envisioned. Several such pairs of images were included in their "Greensward" presentation in 1858.

"The work which has been done in getting ready that part of the park which is now out of sight, underneath the turf, trees and bushes, gravel and water (including the purchased material such as the drain and water pipes), is equivalent to the labor of 1000 men during a period of sixteen years."
Superintendent of Central Park to Gardeners, 1873.

At left, drainage work during the construction of Central Park.

Central Park Construction
One hundred fifty thousand trees and 150,000 shrubs were planted. Seven-and-one-half miles of road, 60 feet wide, the "principal highways," were constructed, originally made of small broken stone "packed firmly as rock." Olmsted later suggested a roadbed of large stones each "eight to 12 inches in length and six to eight in breadth, irregularly rhomboidal in form and moderately soft." They should be set "by hand on the broadest ends, closely, side by side, then crowded or rammed with other smaller stones in the large interstices." In addition, 400 feet of road, 40 feet wide, was built. All the roadways were graded and drained, bedded with unbroken stone, covered with gravel, and rolled. The excavations for the ponds removed 100,000 cubic yards of dirt. This later was used for road and reservoir embankments.

A seven-foot wall of quarried stone was planned for the edge of the mall. This is in evidence today on both the east and west park sides. The final additions were two large bridges (one being the rock over a tunnel, the other of masonry work in connection with a tunnel) and seven smaller timber bridges "as inconspicuous as possible."

Maintenance

The development of an outstanding recreational facility is a considerable achievement, but it's not good enough; it has to be maintained. Maintenance is affected by funds, materials used, community attitude, and individual and public commitment. America is full of public recreational facilities that have, as a result of the combined forces of public apathy and lack of funds, decayed into dysfunctional and dangerous eyesores. Too many communities—tragically but wisely—have had to turn down the gift of a recreational facility because maintenance funds were not a part of the donation.

Philadelphia's Fairmount Park is a verdant expanse of 4110 acres, the world's largest fully maintained city park. Its yearly operating budget is $12,648,735. More than 2500 acres of grass must be cut on a regular basis in the East and West Park area, the 34 outlying parks and squares, and five major parkways under the care and maintenance of the Fairmount Park Commission. Seventy baseball and softball fields, 11 soccer fields, 10 football fields, two cricket fields, two rugby fields, one archery range, one bowling green, 15 miles of designated bikeways (and an estimated 75 miles of undesignated bikeways), and more than 100 miles of bridle paths must be kept in safe and pleasant playing condition in addition to normal ground maintenance.

Building maintenance includes over 400 park structures, including 30 historic buildings, five large recreation centers, the 1500-seat Playhouse-in-the-Park, the 20,000-seat Robin Hood Dell, Memorial Hall, five park police district headquarters and many other buildings. During the past year, 2607 repairs in the areas of carpentry, painting, electric and plumbing work were done in these buildings.

In addition, continual maintenance is required for the many small bridges throughout the park and particularly at the Cobbs Creek and F.D.R. golf courses.

Cleaning up garbage and trash, painting, repairing broken play equipment, and tending grass are four routine maintenance operations.

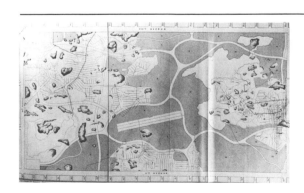

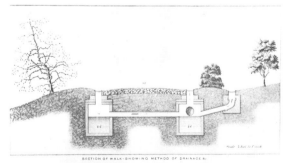

Olmsted was extremely skilled in devising drainage systems for land maintenance. The drawings to the left show the map of drainage pipes for the southern part of Central Park and a detail of the drainage method for a cobbled walk.

These facts highlight two points. First, maintenance should be considered at the ground level of the planning of any recreational facility. For example, certain activities necessitate specialized, frequent, or costly maintenance as opposed to routine upkeep. Second, any recreational facility will be better cared for by the people who use it (thus reducing maintenance frequency and costs) if it genuinely serves their recreational needs.

"*The problem of a park . . . is mainly the reconciliation of adequate beauty of nature in scenery with adequate means in artificial constructions of protecting the conditions of such beauty, and holding it available to the use, in a convenient and orderly way, of those needing it; and in the employment of such means for both purposes, as will make the park steadily gainful of that quality of beauty which comes only with age.*"
A Consideration of the Justifying Values of a Public Park, 1880.

For each of the familiar areas pictured below, try to think of the maintenance operations required and write them in the space provided.

Ecology Maintenance

A "natural" recreation area can be either a man-made product or a piece of untouched nature. In either case, however, the area's particular ecology needs to be maintained. In the case of the man-made park, grass needs to be mowed, facilities painted and repaired, and the like. The maintenance of a truly natural area, though often unseen, is no less critical: most important, the area needs to be kept reasonably free of man's intrusion so that the natural processes that formed it may continue to operate.

The struggle over the Mineral King Valley in the Sierra Nevadas raises an issue becoming more and more common as our population grows and our leisure time and affluence increase, whether the country is better served by scrupulously preventing man's presence from disrupting the ecology of untouched natural areas, or by permitting developers to tamper with nature—diminishing our reserves of land in its natural state—to provide recreational facilities for which there is a genuine demand.

Mineral King Valley is a 300-acre untouched basin area, part of the Sequoia National Game Refuge and the potential site of a Disney Enterprises all-season vacationland. The $36,000,000 development project—which was approved by the Forest Service without public hearings—proposes to "redesign" the valley to make a "natural" recreational environment for 980,000 visitors annually. Construction would include an eight to ten story parking garage, a 1030-room hotel, accommodations for 1000 employees, 22 to 27 ski lifts, and 10 restaurants seating 2350 people. Access needs would be met by a 20-mile, $25,000,000 highway capable of handling 3500 vehicles a day. Disney developers see additional hotels and restaurants being built at the edge of the valley area, on the border of the Sequoia National Park.

The Sierra Club, in a lawsuit against the Forest Service, is protesting the use of public recreational land for private development. The Club maintains that the intrusion of such a complex project, and the construction and activity needed to maintain it, would destroy the present ecology of the area, the most crucial maintenance need of which is to be left largely alone.

So far we have looked at some characteristics of people—what they need—and some characteristics of place—what they permit, encourage, discourage, or prohibit. We have also tried to look at the characteristics of activities themselves. To the right are pictured some common activities, and space for you to add activities that are of special interest or importance to you. By filling in the circles for the appropriate characteristics of each activity, you will create a profile of each activity's overall performance aspects and needs. Pay special attention to the characteristics of the activities you added in comparison with the activities already pictured; it may help you understand the differences between the performance needs of the activities *you* prefer and those of more widely-enjoyed activities.

is for:
infants
toddlers
children
teenagers
adults
the elderly

requires:
extremely specific space or equipment
moderately specific space or equipment
no specific space or equipment

requires a:
small space
medium-sized space
large space

is best served by:
a linear space
a nonlinear space

requires a:
flat terrain
sloped or hilly terrain
steeply sloped or mountainous terrain

requires space:
every block (tot-lot, vest-pocket park)
every neighborhood (neighborhood park/playfield)
once in a small city (city park)
once in a large city (large city central park)
once in a region (regional or national park)

requires:
specific movement or service system
no specific movement or service system

requires:
shelter
safety equipment or restraints
amenities for comfort

is:
strongly affected by time, temperature, weather
generally unaffected by time, temperature, weather

needs a natural-looking setting
is generally unaffected by setting

requires:
space or equipment that needs special maintenance
space or equipment that needs routine maintenance only

47

Locating Your Recreational Resources

The first step in deciding what you need for recreation is determining what you already have. (Remember how many things you wanted to do last year but didn't because the resources were not available?) On these pages are two ways of building up a picture of your recreational opportunities; they both show the same information, but one way shows it as an activity chart, the other as a map with you at its center.

Let's begin by considering availability in terms of time. Time is important as a measure of distance and so as a measure of opportunity. Whether you have a lunch hour, an afternoon, or a weekend will determine what is really available to you. The time distinctions you are working with are: five minutes away (on your block); fifteen minutes away (in your neighborhood); thirty minutes away (in your section of a large city); one hour away (near your city, but an afternoon's trip); three hours away (requiring a day's free time); and one day away (requiring a free weekend).

On the chart, fill in the circles corresponding to how far the listed resources are from your house. Blank lines are left for you to add resources that were left out but that are of special interest to you.

In the diagram of concentric circles, note the same places within the appropriate rings. If you know whether they are north, south, east, or west of where you live and can mark them in approximately the right position, you will also be able to see where each recreational opportunity is in relation to all the others.

Time/distance chart

Where is the nearest:	5 minutes away	15 minutes away	30 minutes away	1 hour away	3 hours away	1 day away	Don't know
playground	○	○	○	○	○	○	○
basketball court	○	○	○	○	○	○	○
tennis court	○	○	○	○	○	○	○
ballfield	○	○	○	○	○	○	○
drinking fountain	○	○	○	○	○	○	○
picnic place	○	○	○	○	○	○	○
pleasant bench	○	○	○	○	○	○	○
street for playing	○	○	○	○	○	○	○
public flower garden	○	○	○	○	○	○	○
climbing tree	○	○	○	○	○	○	○
secluded spot	○	○	○	○	○	○	○
wooded path	○	○	○	○	○	○	○
stream	○	○	○	○	○	○	○
grove of trees	○	○	○	○	○	○	○
duck pond	○	○	○	○	○	○	○
grassy meadow	○	○	○	○	○	○	○
hill	○	○	○	○	○	○	○
waterfall	○	○	○	○	○	○	○
campground	○	○	○	○	○	○	○
fishing lake	○	○	○	○	○	○	○
swimming pool	○	○	○	○	○	○	○
skating rink	○	○	○	○	○	○	○
outdoor theater	○	○	○	○	○	○	○
ski slope	○	○	○	○	○	○	○
zoo	○	○	○	○	○	○	○
_____	○	○	○	○	○	○	○
_____	○	○	○	○	○	○	○

Time/distance map

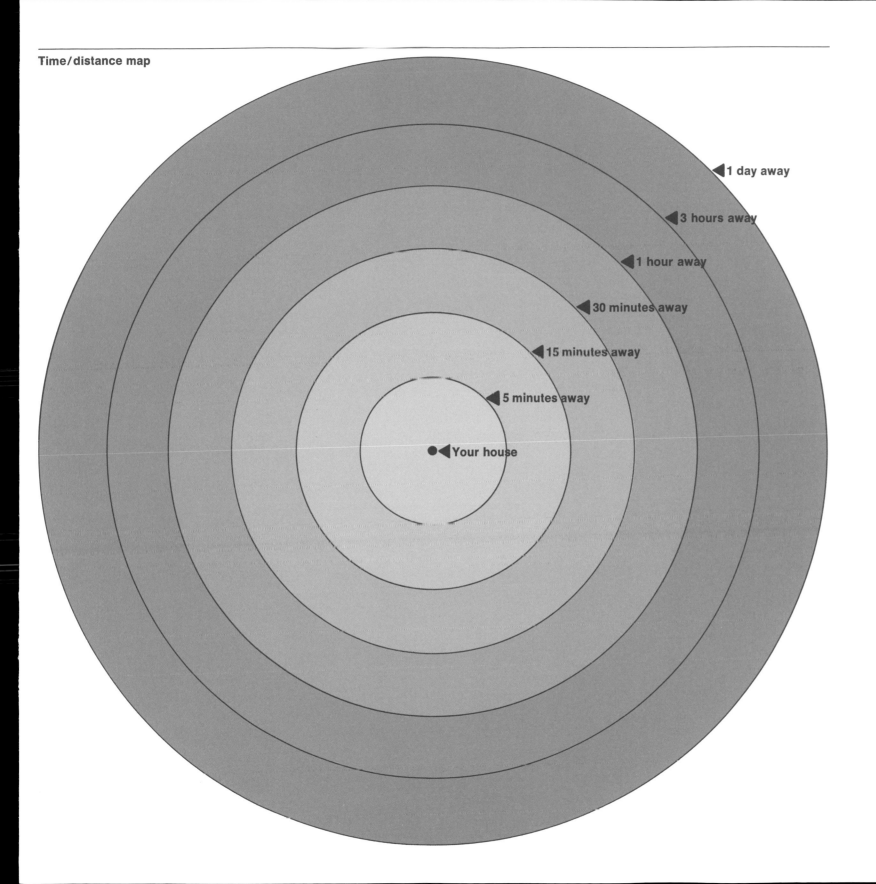

1 day away

3 hours away

1 hour away

30 minutes away

15 minutes away

5 minutes away

● ◀ Your house

Edible Central Park
"Urban Toy," a 6 by 24-foot
scale model of Central Park,
created by Haus-Rucker-Co,
was presented to 10,000 people for an urban feast at the
Central Park Mall in conjunction with the 150th birthday
celebration of Frederick Law
Olmsted. Eaten in less than
90 minutes, the model in-
cluded the entire landscape
of the Park and surrounding
buildings on Central Park
West, North, South and Fifth
Avenue. Skyscrapers on Central Park South towered over
the landscape, created from
300 devil's food, vanilla, and
coconut layer cakes. Park
paths and rocks were made
from pirouette and brownie
chocolate nut cookies. Park
lakes were filled with ched-
dar cheese goldfish crackers.
Building structures, covered
with cream cheese icing,
were constructed from 1,000
slices of white bread. Building interiors and streets were
built from 3,000 slices of
cheese. Facade details, such
as windows and roofs, were
constructed from carrots,
cucumbers, green peppers,
tomatoes, paprika, and basil.
Trees and shrubbery were
made of cauliflower.
Edible architecture is the fifth
"Urban Toy" developed by
Haus-Rucker-Co.

Analyzing One of Your Recreational Resources

Now that you have located all the recreational opportunities that you can get to, enjoy, and get back from in the course of a weekend, let's analyze one of them in terms of the performance components already discussed.

Listed below are questions incorporating performance components, which you will use to judge how well the recreational space you choose actually performs. There are also some questions to help you identify what is unsuccessful about that facility and space to list ways it could be improved.

If you have trouble answering these questions on the basis of your own observations, you could talk to: the designer of the facility, or people at the agency responsible for its construction, to see what needs were being dealt with; people who use the facility; people whom the facility is supposed to serve but who appear not to be using it.

What is the recreational facility you're going to analyze?

_____

Who is this facility for?
- ☐ a block
- ☐ a neighborhood
- ☐ a city
- ☐ a region

- ☐ infants
- ☐ toddlers
- ☐ children
- ☐ teenagers
- ☐ adults
- ☐ the elderly

How many people can it serve comfortably?

_____

Can it serve all these people at once?
- ☐ yes
- ☐ no

Do different groups of people use it at different times of the day or week?
- ☐ yes
- ☐ no

Is it well located for the people it serves?
- ☐ yes
- ☐ no

Is it safe and comfortable?
- ☐ yes
- ☐ no

If not, what would it take to make it so?

_____

Does it have:
- ☐ adequate parking
- ☐ bicycle racks
- ☐ night lighting
- ☐ drinking fountain
- ☐ snack bar
- ☐ toilets

Is it well maintained?
- ☐ yes
- ☐ no

What do you think are the five most popular activities of the people who use this facility, including yourself?

_____

_____

_____

_____

What activities does this facility encourage or permit? Which ones does it discourage or prohibit?

Encourages

_____

_____

_____

Discourages

_____

_____

_____

Can activities appropriate to both the young and old take place there?
- ☐ yes
- ☐ no
- ☐ not needed

Are facilities for both individual and group activities provided?
- ☐ yes
- ☐ no
- ☐ not needed

Are both specific and nonspecific spaces provided?

- ☐ yes
- ☐ no
- ☐ not needed

Does it have small spaces?

- ☐ yes
- ☐ no
- ☐ not needed

Does it have large spaces?

- ☐ yes
- ☐ no
- ☐ not needed

Does it provide areas for both linear and non-linear activities?

- ☐ yes
- ☐ no
- ☐ not needed

Are there spaces which permit and encourage inactive as well as active forms of recreation?

- ☐ yes
- ☐ no
- ☐ not needed

What different kinds of terrain are provided?

- ☐ flat
- ☐ gently sloping
- ☐ rolling or hilly
- ☐ steeply sloping
- ☐ mountainous

What distinctive natural features are there?

- ☐ hills
- ☐ water
- ☐ cliffs
- Others

_____

_____

_____

When was this facility planned and built?

_____

Have users' needs changed significantly since then or since the facility's most recent renovation?

- ☐ yes
- ☐ no

If yes, how?

_____

_____

Would it be easy to make changes in this facility in response to changed needs?

- ☐ yes
- ☐ no

Do *you* use this recreational resource often?

- ☐ yes
- ☐ no

Would you use it more often if it was closer to you?

- ☐ yes
- ☐ no

If it had different things in it?

- ☐ yes
- ☐ no

Do you feel comfortable with the other people who use it?

- ☐ yes
- ☐ no

What do *you* do there?

_____

_____

What are the things you can't do there that you would like to do?

_____

_____

Can you do these things somewhere else?

- ☐ yes
- ☐ no

List the five things about this recreational facility that you most like.

_____

_____

_____

_____

List the five things that you most dislike.

_____

_____

_____

_____

Do the good things outweigh the bad things?

- ☐ yes
- ☐ no

List the changes or improvements you feel should be made in order of their importance.

_____

_____

_____

_____

How many of these changes would have to be made before you would call this space a good recreational resource?

_____

Developing a Program

Having thought about how one of the recreational spaces you use actually performs, now let's develop a program for an ideal recreational space. This will require that we analyze people and activity needs and that we determine space requirements based on these needs, again by making use of performance components.

Before we do anything else we have to decide whose needs we're developing this program to satisfy.

Is it for you and

☐   your family
☐   your neighborhood
☐   a section of your city
☐   your entire city

About how many people will use this space

_____ often

_____ occasionally

_____ once in a while

What percentage of its use will be by people

_____ individually

_____ in families or small groups

_____ in large groups

What do you think the percentage of users in each age group will be?

_____ 0-3 years old

_____ 3-6

_____ 6-11

_____ 11-18

_____ 18-30

_____ 30-50

_____ 50-65

_____ 65 and older

Do you need spaces for both inactive and active forms of recreation?

☐   yes
☐   no

For free-form as well as organized types of activities?

☐   yes
☐   no

For linear as well as nonlinear activities?

☐   yes
☐   no

List the ten most important activities that you feel space and facilities should be provided for.

_____

_____

_____

_____

_____

_____

_____

_____

_____

_____

On the basis of your answers above, you can start to choose the kinds of spaces that will meet your requirements.

List the kinds of different spaces that you feel should be there, describing them in terms of qualities rather than function. For example: a medium-sized hilly space; a large flat space; a shady linear space, etc.

_____

_____

_____

_____

_____

What specific facilities will be needed? List them in order of importance.

_____

_____

_____

_____

_____

Add any cultural or educational resources that your analysis of users' needs suggests you should have (for example, a zoo, a bandshell, or a sound system).

_____

_____

_____

Where would you place your recreational facility relative to the area it serves?
- ☐ in the center
- ☐ along an edge
- ☐ in a corner

Have you considered the location of existing recreational resources in making that decision?
- ☐ yes
- ☐ no

Have you considered the location of natural features and resources?
- ☐ yes
- ☐ no

What separate movement systems—such as walking paths, bicycle paths, service roads—does your program demand?

_____

_____

_____

What specific safety features or restraints will this facility need?

_____

_____

_____

Would your program utilize the space
- ☐ day and night
- ☐ all day
- ☐ most of the day
- ☐ some of the day

Can the spaces you've described meet peak-hour demands for use?
- ☐ yes
- ☐ no

Are your choices of spaces and facilities economical considering the periods of decreased use?
- ☐ yes
- ☐ no

Would you specify a lighting system for night use or safety?
- ☐ yes
- ☐ no

Does your program consider the different temperature, seasonal, weather, and climatic conditions of your location?
- ☐ yes
- ☐ no

How much real construction will be required as opposed to utilizing "found spaces" or land essentially as is?
- ☐ a great deal
- ☐ a lot
- ☐ some
- ☐ only a little

Does your program involve heavy maintenance commitments or the frequent replacement of expensive equipment?
- ☐ yes
- ☐ no

Would your recreational area be flexible enough to change if users' needs should change in the future?
- ☐ yes
- ☐ no

In a few pages you will have a chance to apply your ideas to the actual design of a recreational space.

Identifying Recreational Possibilities

Too often we ignore potential recreational resources simply because they don't fit our preconceptions about what a recreational facility should look like. We are so familiar with tot-lots, vest-pocket parks, playgrounds, and city and regional parks, as well as special facilities such as zoos, botanical gardens, and outdoor theaters, that we just don't recognize the potential recreational spaces all around us.

Often we don't see these spaces because they are too familiar—they are places that we use or experience every day for nonrecreational purposes and that we automatically assume have no other function—for example, sidewalks, streets, alleys, or parking lots. Other spaces that we might not notice are spaces that we usually consider "dead spaces." They are

New Thoughts for Old Spaces

In high density urban areas it is especially important to recognize the versatility of existing space and substitute new activities in old activity areas.

A study of the Meridian Hill area of Washington, D.C., disclosed that certain definable activity patterns of what people were inclined to do existed among the residents. An investigation into the physical properties of the community revealed that there were existing underutilized spaces which could be used for recreation. A back street alley system of play areas, walkways, sitting areas, and small gardens was proposed, to be used in conjunction with a day care center and youth training center. Its development would provide self-help job experience in addition to utilizing a much needed space resource. A block-long residential street which carried a minimum of traffic and was used mainly as a pedestrian route to local shops and bus stops was to be closed and developed as a play street. Parking compounds at both ends, plantings, benches and portable play equipment completed the proposal.

Street

Lot

Parking lot

not used for anything at all and have become sanctioned as wasteland in our minds. What about the fenced-in area under a freeway interchange? Or the generous medians on some residential streets and parkways? How many vacant lots are nearby? There are also potential recreational resources that we don't see because they are not very accessible or have unpleasant associations—for example, abandoned or unused spaces near

factories or railroad yards, or the high-grassed fields or undeveloped marshy areas near streams, lakes, or canals.

Some of these places could be turned into part-time or full-time recreational resources. Making use of presently under-utilized space is just about the easiest way to add to your recreational opportunities.

Below are photographs of some of the underused spaces described above. Under each, list the recreational activities that you think these places could be used for. After you have made your list, write the most important things that need to be changed or considered in order to make the space a workable recreational resource in terms of the component factors we've previously discussed.

Factory yard

Waterside

Median strip, Underpass

Recreation as Education
New Haven, Connecticut, offers an example of how municipal park and recreation departments may function in the area of environmental education. This city's park and recreation commission sponsors a 40-acre nature recreation center, which offers a laboratory for guided field trips, courses, and workshops concerned with natural history, wildlife preservation, weather, astronomy, geology, and geography. Thousands of students on all grade levels, as well as some students in special education classes and a unique bilingual program are served in a program jointly sponsored by the New Haven Park and Recreation Commission and the city's school board.

Six ranger-naturalists teach courses in various aspects of nature and ecology, and are assisted by volunteers provided by the New Haven Nature Recreation Association. The center also provides field study opportunities and work periods for students at nearby Southern Connecticut State College. Plans are under way to expand this program by adding other nature centers and day camps, including a seashore center, to be concerned with marine biology and ecology.

Choosing among Recreational Possibilities

Now that you've identified a whole new range of potential recreational resources, let's begin the process of choosing those that are best for your particular program.

In the circle map, mark down all the potential recreational sites that you can think of within the appropriate time/distance ring of five minutes, fifteen minutes, half an hour, or one hour. It will be helpful to you later if you can put them in the right direction relative to your house at the center, but it's not critical. Because you'll probably come up with so many, you may want to use a symbol code like the one at the right.

Time/distance map

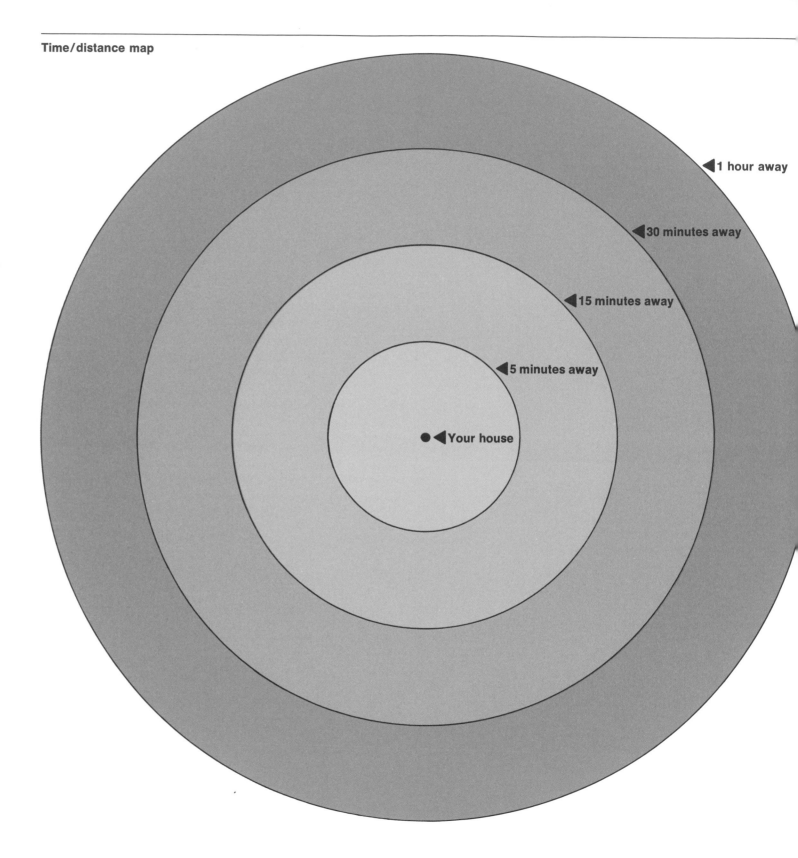

1 hour away

30 minutes away

15 minutes away

5 minutes away

Your house

Symbol code

Street	
Block	
Underpass	
Lot	
Median strip	
Lake	
River	
Hill	
Grassy area	
Wooded area	

After charting more possible spaces than you could ever use or need, you will have to make some decisions about which potential spaces will perform according to the needs of your program. In the chart at the right—which is like the chart on page 48—fill in the circles corresponding to the time/distance away from your house that you feel each recreational resource should exist.

After charting how close to you each listed resource should be able to be found, you're almost ready to choose which of the potential spaces you've identified best meet the demands of your program. On the next page are some questions for you to ask yourself about the potential sites you have identified. These questions will help you confirm that you're making the best use of each potential site. If the places you have chosen are not dealt with here, try to think of similar questions that could be applied to your sites.

Time/distance chart

How near should there be a:	5 minutes away	15 minutes away	30 minutes away	1 hour away	Don't know
playground	○	○	○	○	○
basketball court	○	○	○	○	○
tennis court	○	○	○	○	○
ballfield	○	○	○	○	○
drinking fountain	○	○	○	○	○
picnic place	○	○	○	○	○
pleasant bench	○	○	○	○	○
street for playing	○	○	○	○	○
public flower garden	○	○	○	○	○
climbing tree	○	○	○	○	○
secluded spot	○	○	○	○	○
wooded path	○	○	○	○	○
stream	○	○	○	○	○
grove of trees	○	○	○	○	○
duck pond	○	○	○	○	○
grassy meadow	○	○	○	○	○
hill	○	○	○	○	○
waterfall	○	○	○	○	○
campground	○	○	○	○	○
fishing lake	○	○	○	○	○
swimming pool	○	○	○	○	○
skating rink	○	○	○	○	○
outdoor theater	○	○	○	○	○
ski slope	○	○	○	○	○
zoo	○	○	○	○	○
————	○	○	○	○	○
————	○	○	○	○	○

Questions	Street	Lot or Block	Waterside
	Who would this space serve?	Who would this space serve?	Who would this area serve?
	Is it big enough for them?	Is it big enough for them?	Is it big enough for them?
	Is it well located for them?	Is it well located for them?	Is it well located for them?
	If there is a lot of traffic, could the street be closed and traffic rerouted?	Is it adequately screened or protected from the street or existing adjacent activity?	What would you be able to do there: wade, swim, sail toy boats, sail a boat, row a boat, dive, skin-dive, fish, waterski, surf, ice skate in the winter?
	All of the time or just during certain hours?	Are there amenities nearby, such as drinking water, refreshments, shelter, and toilets?	Would the facility you have in mind be used mostly by children, teenagers and adults, or families?
	Could you limit the hours for street-destined traffic, such as essential deliveries or public services?	If not, could they be provided?	Is the land at the water's edge privately or publicly owned?
		Is extensive construction needed to adapt this area to your needs?	
	Are the buildings far away from actively-used areas, or are windows and damageable surfaces protected?	Would the construction be of a permanent or flexible nature?	Is the water ready to be used or is it dangerously polluted?
			Is the body of water a pond, lake, stream, or river?
	Would utilizing this street for recreational purposes be detrimental to the present functions of the street or to the quality of life that the street now offers its residents?	Is the land presently private, public, commercial, industrial, residential? Occupied or abandoned?	Did you choose it because there was no other useable water in the area or for its ability to fulfill specific aspects of your program?
		Who might finance the development of this space —individuals, a foundation, the city, or the state?	
	If so, could you use a different street?	Who would be responsible for maintenance?	During what hours would you have this facility open for use?
	Why is this street a valuable asset to your program?	What factors led you to choose this space over other potential spaces?	Which of the following would you have to provide: parking, revised public transportation routes, a lifeguard, controlled access, refreshments, first aid, boat rental, changing lockers, equipment storage?
	What are its disadvantages?		
	How might you resolve them?		What would actually have to be built to prepare this waterside for use as the recreational resource you envision?
			Would your proposals have any detrimental effects on the ecology of the area?

If, with the help of these questions, you have been able to decide definitely on the potential spaces you would choose to activate, you can use the circle diagram on the right-hand page to chart your total proposed recreational system, that is, the recreational facilities that already exist combined with the areas you would like to see developed. We suggest that you use a different colored pencil or pen to distinguish between existing recreational areas and the facilities that you have proposed. The symbol code is to help you chart some of your *existing* resources in the same way that you charted your *potential* resources on page 56.

Time/distance map

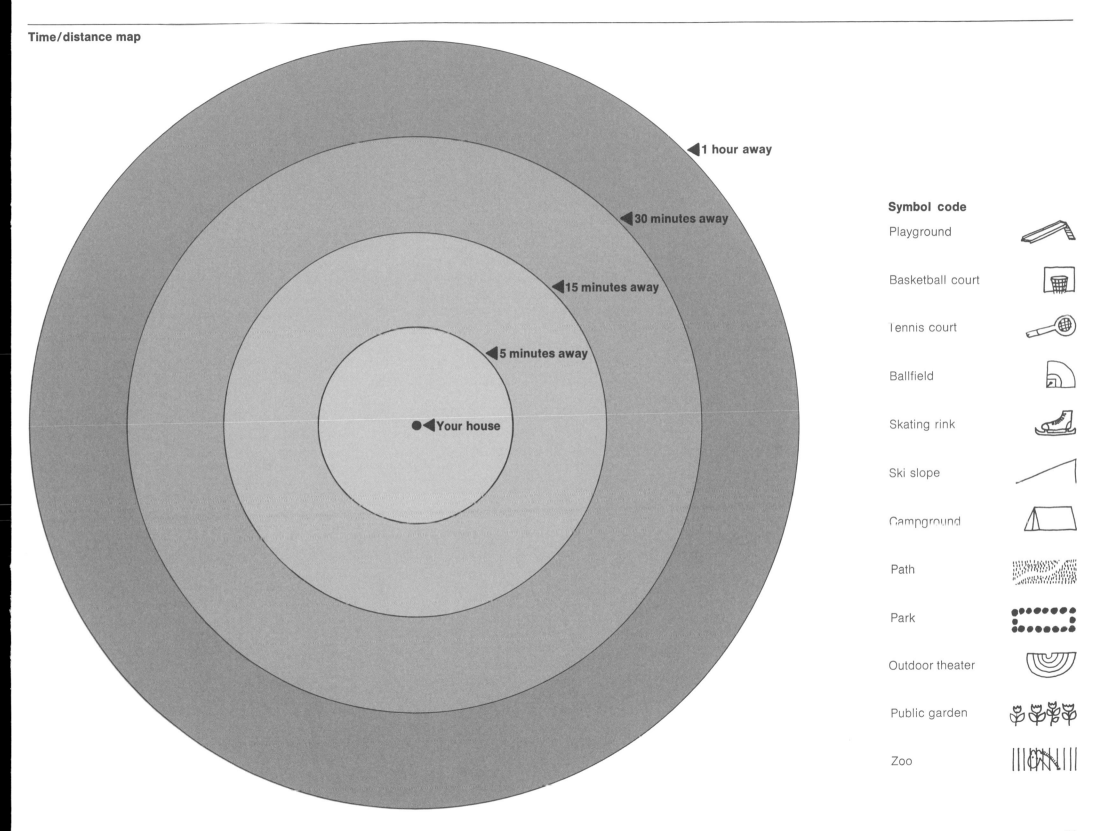

1 hour away

30 minutes away

15 minutes away

5 minutes away

Your house

Symbol code

Playground

Basketball court

Tennis court

Ballfield

Skating rink

Ski slope

Campground

Path

Park

Outdoor theater

Public garden

Zoo

Developing Recreational Resources

On the preceding pages you have identified some potential recreational resources by program content, availability, and an analysis of performance features. On the following pages you will develop a few of them. The next five pages contain drawings of some characteristic types of potential recreational spaces: a street; a sidewalk; a small lot; a city block; and a waterside area. There is room to write in any specific characteristics of these spaces that you identified on the last two pages and that you feel are important in trying to activate these spaces for recreational use.

Between pages 64 and 65 are drawings of everything from trees, benches, and rowboats to basketball and tennis courts and sandboxes. They are scaled to the drawings of the empty spaces. Punch out the drawings and move them around to discover the best placement and combinations of recreational facilities. If there are not enough labels, or if they do not suit your needs because of their shape or size, simply draw or write in what you need.

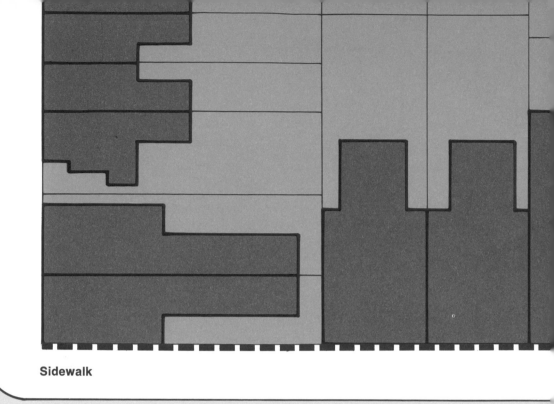

Sidewalk

Street

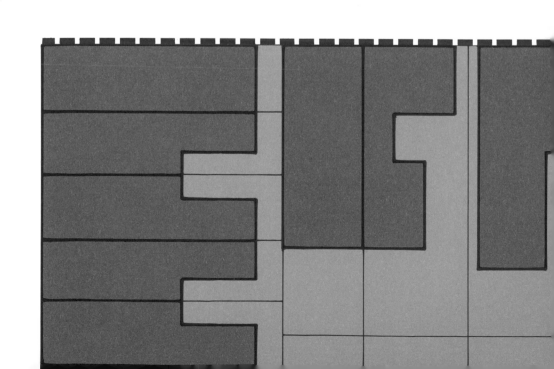

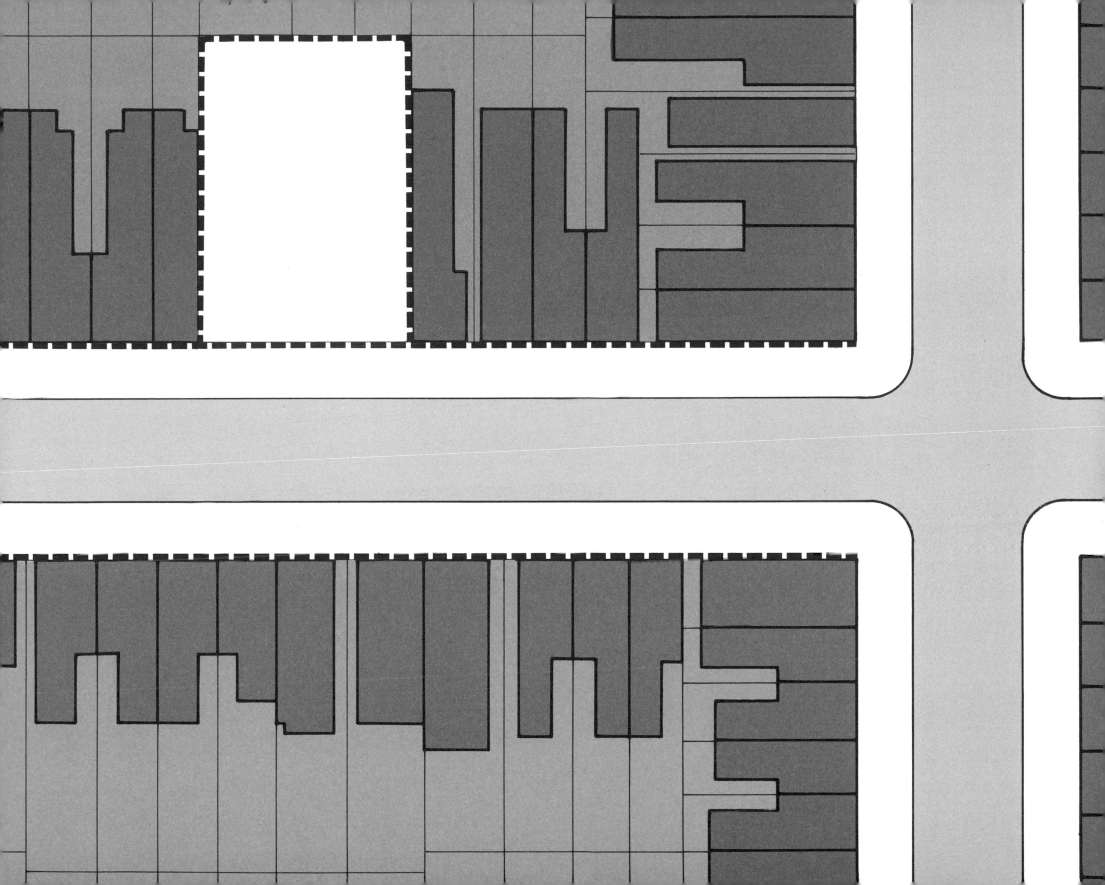

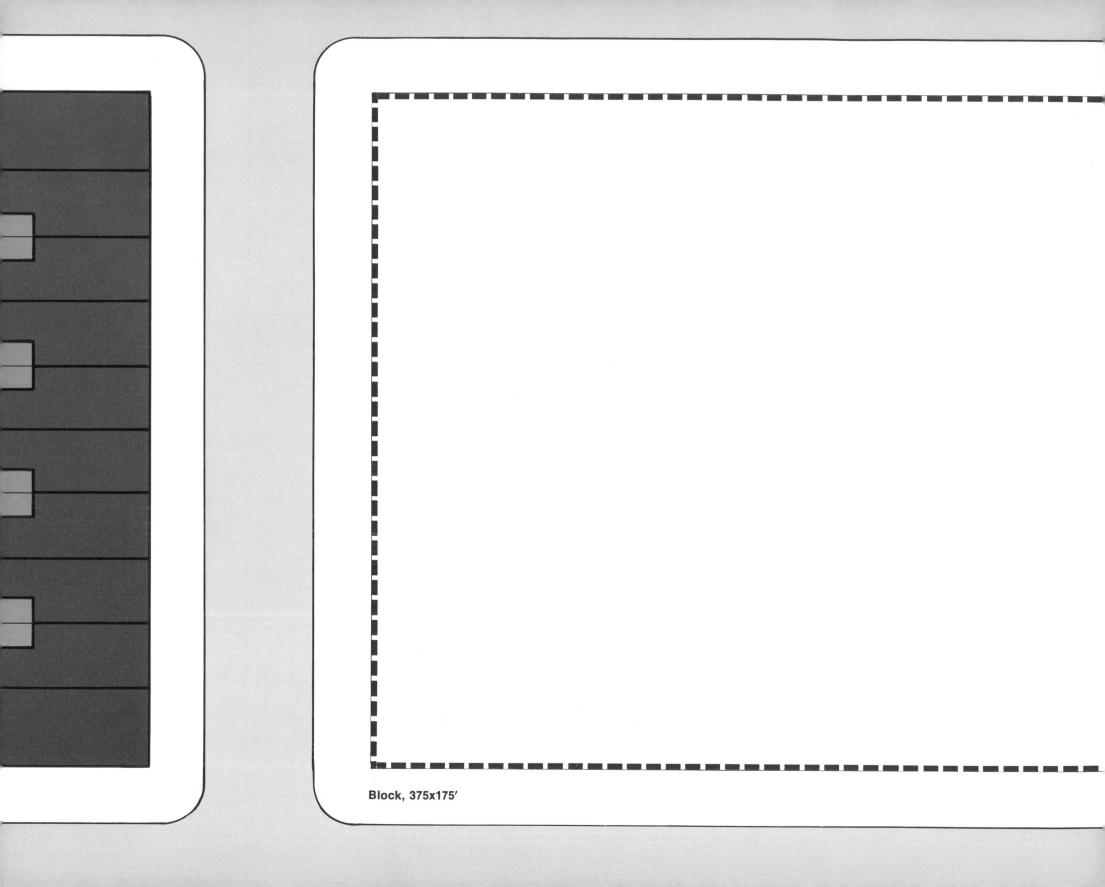

Block, 375x175′

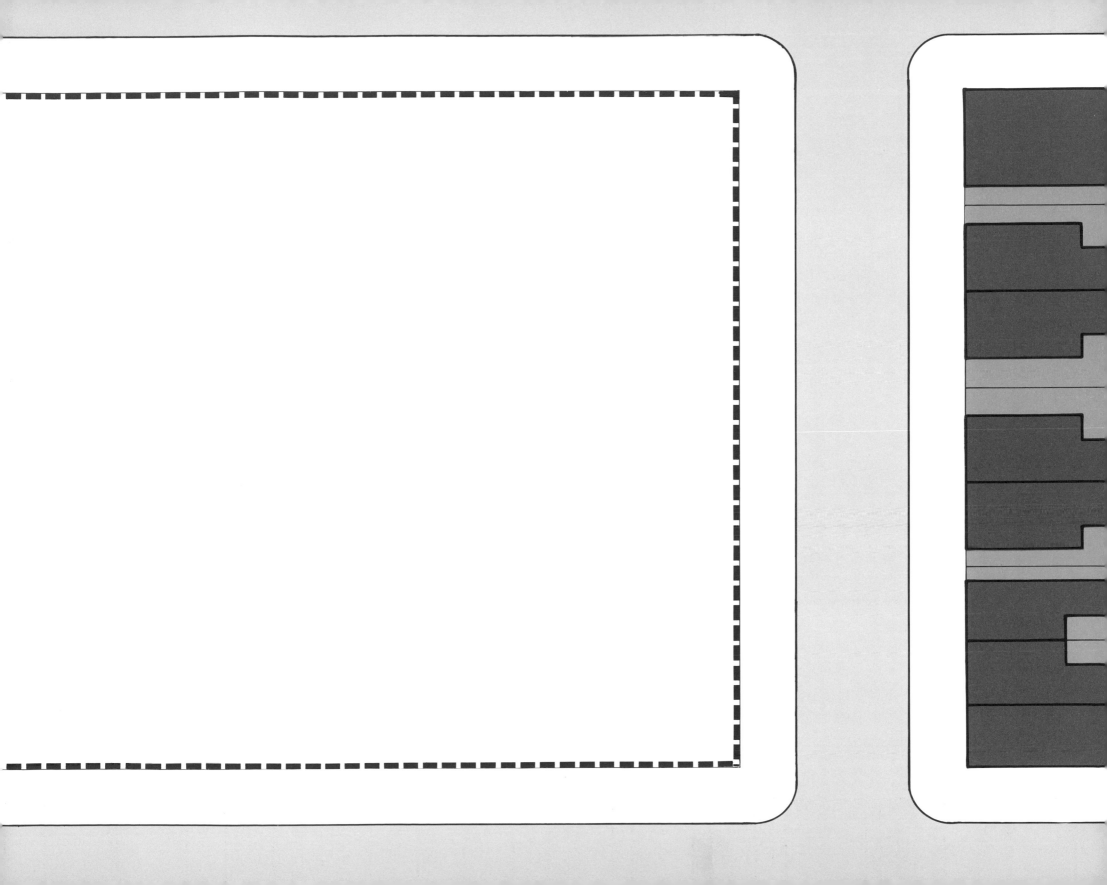

Waterside

Basketball courts

A full-size football field is 360 by 160 feet, not including sidelines. Too big for us to give you as a label, it would fit in the empty city block on pages 62 and 63, but no room would be left for anything else. If you think that the needs of your program would best be met by turning the entire block into a football field, you may draw it in using the scale.

Baseball field

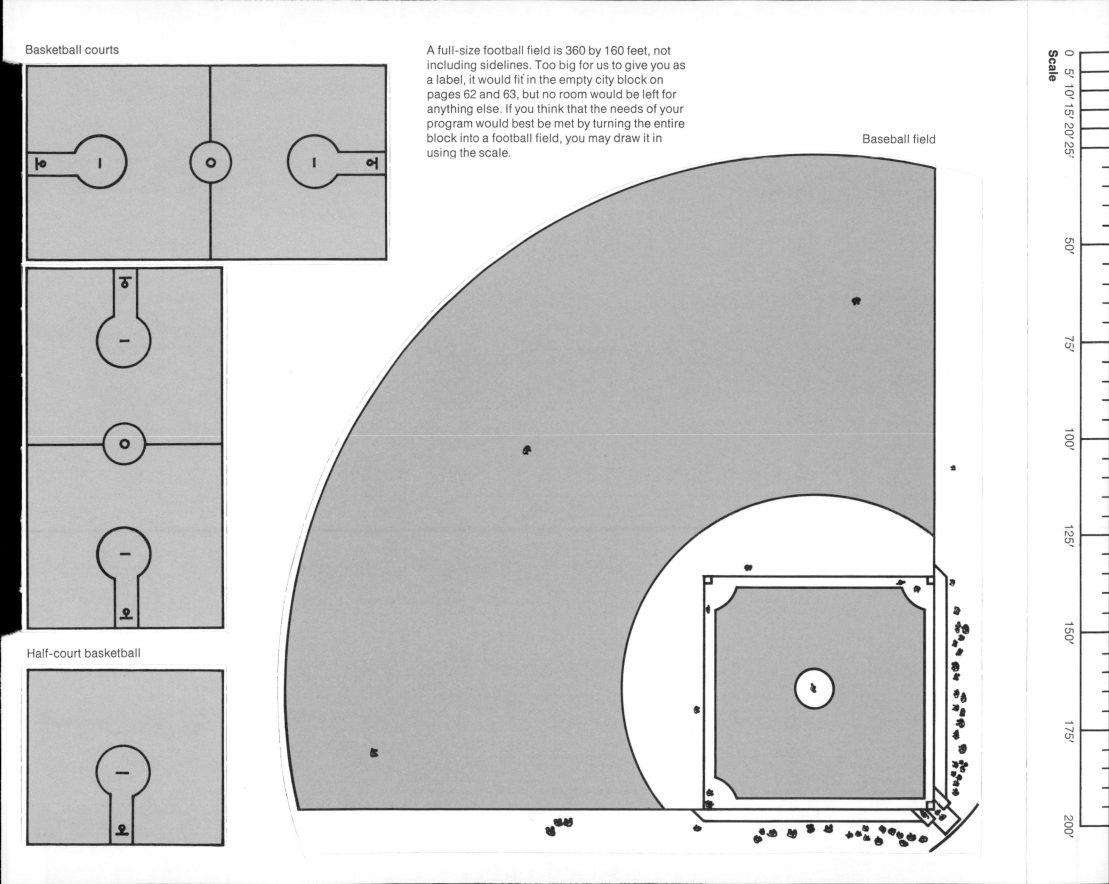

Half-court basketball

pages 62 and 63

Scale

0 5' 10' 15' 20' 25'

50'

75'

100'

125'

150'

175'

200'

Trees

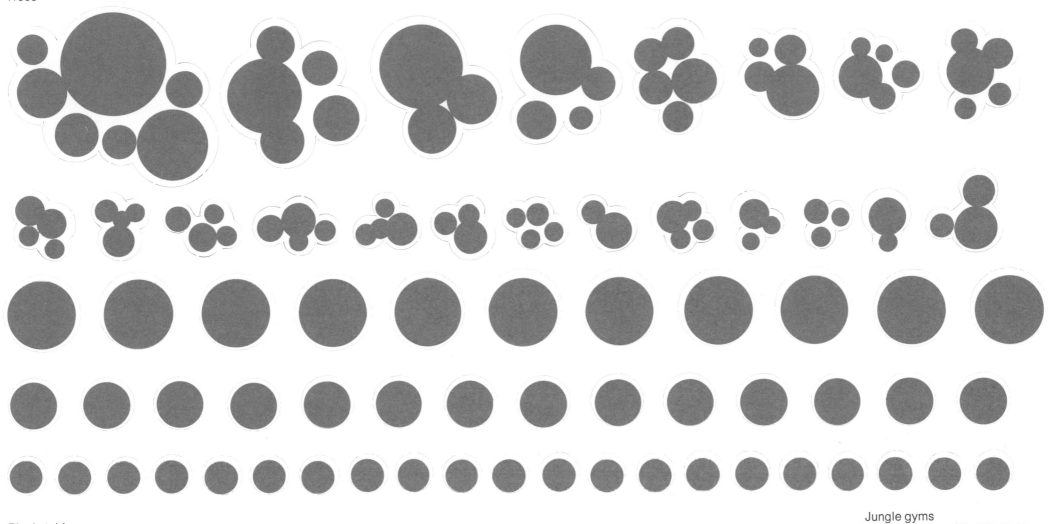

Picnic tables

Jungle gyms

Merry-go-rounds

Benches

Fountains

Amphitheater

Sandboxes

Wading pools

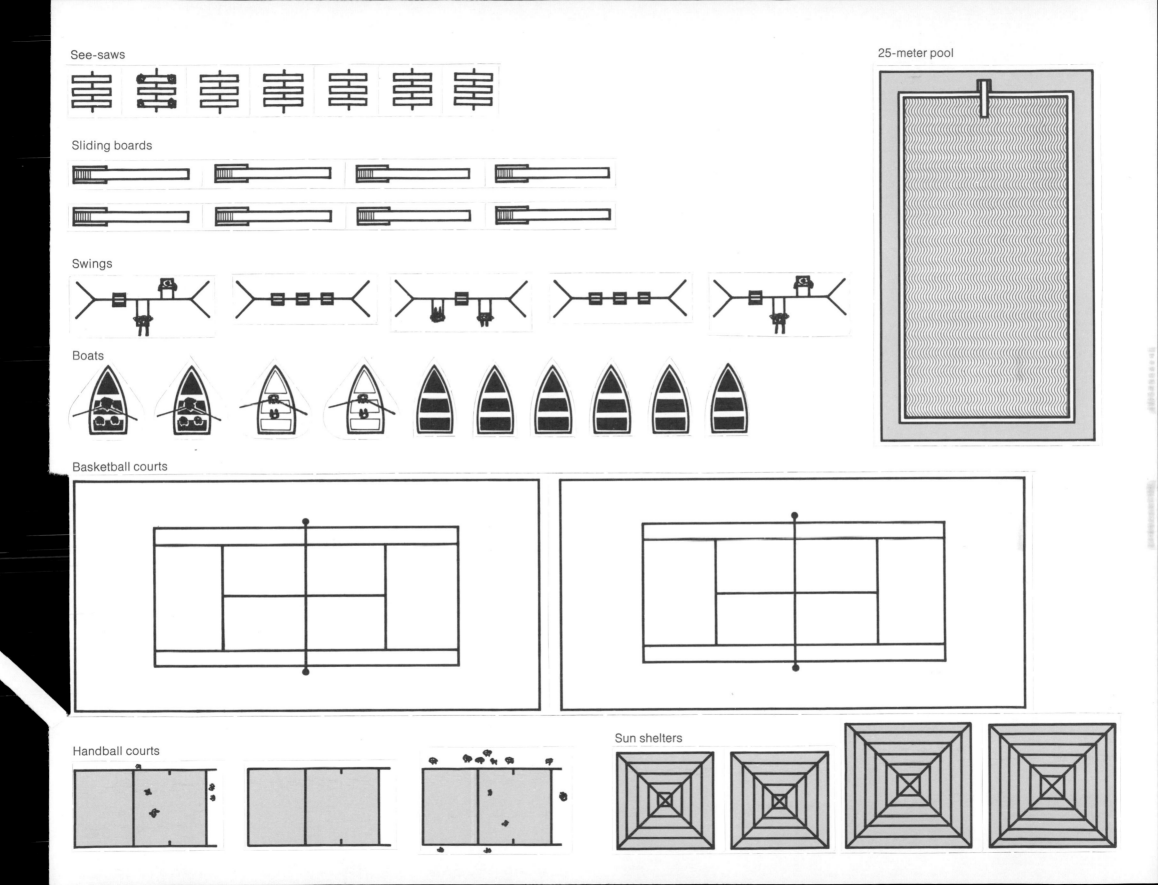

See-saws

Sliding boards

Swings

Boats

25-meter pool

Basketball courts

Handball courts

Sun shelters

Afterword

The Nature of Recreation has been concerned with your abilities to:

Understand your recreational needs and desires — what you want;

See the relationship between recreational modes and physical space and form as well as opportunities for recreational activities in existing places;

Realize the major difference between performance demands and product proliferation and recognize the former as the viable tool for recreational planning;

Develop your skills to articulate programs of constructive demands.

The Nature of Recreation has used the Olmsted example as well as a wide range of facts, ideas, and illustrations, to enrich your encounter with the definition, necessity, and availability of recreation.

The appendix which follows fills out this definition and allows you to explore further the ideas and opinions of a selected group of professionals. It also includes some street games and children's game chants, game space diagrams, and an informal Olmsted bibliography.

Appendix

An Olmsted Bibliography

In their first suburban plan, for Riverside, six miles from Chicago, Olmsted and Vaux established the foundation for better community design. Rejecting the uniform grid-system layout of the time, Olmsted shaped the lots and streets to natural topography and to the meanders of the Des Plains River bordering the site. Roadways were depressed, to avoid breaking the visual flow of the gently rolling landscape, seemingly natural clusters of trees were planted, common greens were scattered throughout the project, and business and pleasure traffic were separated. Riverside has managed to maintain its rural character for almost a century, despite the pattern of urban growth surrounding it.

"The demands of suburban life, with reference to civilized refinement, are not to be a retrogression from, but an advance upon, those which are characteristic of town life, and . . . no great town can long exist without great suburbs."
To the Riverside Improvement Company, 1868.

Rather than a complete bibliography of writings *by* Frederick Law Olmsted, this is rather a list of collections of selected writings and currently available books *about* him and his work. Many of them contain a traditional bibliography of his writings.

Civilizing American Cities: A Selection of Frederick Law Olmsted's Writings on City Landscapes
S. B. Sutton, editor
Cambridge, The M.I.T. Press, 1971.
This book reprints Olmsted's reports on San Francisco, Buffalo, Chicago, Montreal, Boston, Berkeley, Riverside (Illinois), the Brooklyn parkway, the streets of the twenty-third and twenty-fourth wards of New York City, and his long article, "Public Parks and the Enlargement of Towns."

Frederick Law Olmsted and the American Environmental Tradition
Albert Fein
New York, Braziller, 1972.
The text of this book places Olmsted's thought within the context of the nineteenth century social ideals but is not as helpful in showing how his designs transformed those ideals into an environmental reality. The reproduction of his plans is extremely poor.

Frederick Law Olmsted: Landscape Architect, 1822-1903
Frederick Law Olmsted Jr. and Theodora Kimball, editors
New York, Benjamin Blom, 1970.
A reissue of the original 1928 two-book edition published under the title, *Frederick Law Olmsted: Forty Years of Landscape Architecture,* this book contains official reports on Central Park as well as autobiographical writings by Olmsted and critical comments by the editors.

Frederick Law Olmsted's New York
Elizabeth Barlow (text) and William Alex (illustrative portfolio)
New York, Praeger, in association with the Whitney Museum of American Art, 1972.
A vivid account of Olmsted's hesitant decision to become a landscape architect and his subsequent work in New York City. The text on Central Park is thorough, but his other New York work is dealt with too briefly considering its importance.

Frederick Law Olmsted Sr.: Founder of Landscape Architecture in America
Julius Gy. Fabos, Gordon T. Milde, V. Michael Weinmayer
Amherst, University of Massachusetts Press, 1968.
A beautifully designed and printed book, which includes a selection of quotes from Olmsted's writing, a detailed chronology of his life, bibliography and list of projects. Unfortunately, the text is brief and not helpful in understanding the illustrations.

Landscape into Cityscape: Frederick Law Olmsted's Plans for a Greater New York City
Albert Fein, editor
Ithaca, Cornell University Press, 1968.
The reports for Olmsted's New York work are included in this book, which also contains a good introduction and interesting illustrations.

Olmsted in Chicago
Victoria Post Ranney
Chicago, Donnelley and Sons, 1972.
A brief, informative text on Olmsted's Chicago work with good photographs from both the nineteenth and twentieth centuries.

In his work for Stanford University, Olmsted pointed out the folly of miming English and New England collegiate architecture in the climate of California. Accordingly, he designed a system of small, enclosed spaces protected from the heat and wind.

"In the plan for a great University in California ideals must be given up that have been planted by all that we have found agreeable . . . in the outward aspect of Eastern and English colleges. If we are to look for types of buildings and arrangements suitable to the climate of California it will rather be in those founded by the wiser men of Syria, Greece, Italy, and Spain."
Letter to Leland Stanford, 1886.

A Recreational Bibliography

Diminishing urban space and the exorbitant cost of land generally precludes the possibility of the city or state acquiring new land for recreational use. Imaginative uses have to be found for existing open space. Sometimes, it is simply a question of recognizing that there *is* open space. Present uses and misuses of land, especially in decayed urban neighborhoods, make the potential for putting open space to recreational use seem much smaller than it really is.

The following books deal with some of the most recent and thought-provoking ideas about outdoor space and its recreational use. They survey current trends and forecast directions for the future. Some express their ideas through philosophy, while others offer specific design solutions. All reflect to a greater or lesser degree, however, the conviction that only through imaginative innovation will our recreational needs be met.

Design with Nature
Ian L. McHarg
Garden City, Doubleday, 1969.
198 pp., 8x8", $5.95.

Ecology is a much abused term these days, used to define a broad range of ideas and causes. However, an essential component in any area of environmental planning is an understanding of the fundamentals of ecology: what constitutes a balanced and self-renewing environment; what the necessary ingredients are for man's biological prosperity, social cooperation, and spiritual stimulation.

This book provides a stunning overview of those aspects necessary to man's relationship with nature. It demonstrates with specific examples how this knowledge should be applied to actual environments, *"to caring for natural areas, like swamps, lakes, rivers, to choosing sites for further urban settlements to reestablishing human norms and life-furthering objectives in metropolitan areas."*

The graphics and photographs add an additional element of cohesion and clarity; the text is clear, humble, and concise. This is an essential primer for all ages and for all points of view concerned with human activity, with the world around us, and with our relationship to it and to ourselves.

Outdoor Recreation Trends

Bureau of Outdoor Recreation
Washington, D.C., U.S. Government Printing
Office, 1967.
24 pp., 9x11½", 40¢.

Trends shown by a Bureau of Outdoor Recreation survey of participation in outdoor recreation activities. Many of this book's statistics appear in the marginalia of *The Nature of Recreation*.

"Our outdoor recreation demands have become imperative. To meet the forseeable demands, we have embarked upon preparation of a long-range and continuing Nationwide Outdoor Recreation Plan."

"This booklet details certain of the intense summertime recreation activity which the Bureau of Outdoor Recreation of the Department of the Interior has found in preparing the Nationwide Outdoor Recreation Plan. Evaluation of this data and recommendations to meet the needs which the figures indicate will be a significant part of the forthcoming Plan."

Open Space for Human Needs

Edited by Donald Canty in conjunction with
Kevin Lynch, Marvin Clive, and Carl Feiss
Washington, D.C., The National Urban Coalition,
1965.
52 pp., 9¾x13¼".

This report, prepared for the Department of Housing and Urban Development, seeks to provide guidance to state and local officials in planning and designing closer-in spaces which are not totally committed to traditional recreational activities. The study's approach to open space design from the viewpoint of directly meeting human needs should be one facet of planning a total system of metropolitan open space.

Examples of open space planning include analyses of Anacostia and Meridian Hill, two Washington, D.C., communities, and design solutions for an alley system, street closing, and play facilities.

Open Space for People: Acquisition, Conservation, Creation and Design

Edited by Mildred F. Schmertz
Washington, D.C., American Institute of Architects, 1972. Available from the publisher.
111 pp., 11¼x9¼".

This is a report from the 1970 International Conference on the Commission on Town Planning. It contains twelve papers from such speakers as Chloethiel Woodard Smith, Luben Tonev, Carl Feiss, Matthew Rockwell, Antonio Perpina Sebria, Jean Henri Calsat, and James H. Scheuer. It covers such subjects as long range planning and acquisition of open space in both urban and rural areas, estimating future recreational needs, and the feasibility of current solutions. It presents future design proposals and analyzes existing recreational areas.

"All the photographs and drawings in this report have been chosen to make the following simple points: open space is essential for man's most important needs; we are wearing out what we have, including the great parks which have been preserved as a legacy from our past; we are squandering the rest through inadequate advance acquisition; we must conserve what is left for the future; we must find ways of creating and acquiring new kinds of open space within the imperatives of our technology."

A "people's park" playground built for the Bromley Heath Housing Project in Boston. Designed by MIT students, parks like these can be erected in a day with student and community participation on neglected neighborhood open space.

Leisure

Illinois Institute of Technology
Chicago, Institute of Design Press, 1970.
79 pp., 8½x11".

"As a group predetermined to study the problem of recreation and leisure in the next decade, we decided that before any environmental conclusions could be recommended we first had to explain and clarify our concept of man and leisure.

" 'The most useless and wasteful effort is that of a design and engineering team that with great speed, precision and elegance turns out drawings for the wrong product,' writes Peter Drucker. Further, as a result of our own confusion over the concepts of leisure, recreation and work we found that upon coming to an understanding of the problems therein, our most important task was to communicate our knowledge to others."

"The leisure problem is fundamental. Having to decide what we shall do with our leisure is inevitably forcing us to re-examine the purpose of human existence, and to ask what fulfillment really means. . . . This involves a comprehensive survey of human possibilities and methods of realizing them; it also implies a survey of the obstacles to their realization."
Julian Huxley, *The Future of Man,* quoted in *Leisure.*

" In recreation, we are witnessing a migration away from the highly anticipated and planned yearly vacation to a more rhythm[ical] and 'natural' long weekend style of recreation."

"An idea that seems to have a great appeal to us is to extend the use of the traditional American farm for recreation. The kinds of interesting experiences on a typical farm are not only fun but educational, particularly for second generation urbanites and children."

Small Urban Spaces: The Philosophy, Design, Sociology and Politics of Vest-Pocket Parks
Edited by Whitney North Seymour Jr.
New York, New York University Press, 1969.
198 pp., 7¼ x 9¼", $6.50.

This is a collection of both ideals and how-to-do-it details about new ways to use small urban spaces creatively. Articles by Lewis Mumford, Jane Jacobs, Robert Zion, Lady Allen of Hurtwood, Paul Friedberg, Eve Asner, and others discuss neighborhood and vest-pocket parks, the advantages and design details of midtown parks such as Paley Park, system design for play equipment, adventure playgrounds, and implementation of parks in general.

Paley Park, Fifty-third Street, near Fifth Avenue, New York City.

"It may be defined as a small park (50x100'), yet big enough in essence to reaffirm the dignity of the human being. It is a pool of space removed from the flow of traffic (including pedestrian traffic) enclosed, and sheltered from noise. Preferably, it is a space between buildings, benefiting from the shelter of neighboring structures, the type of space that is now most commonly used as a parking lot."
Robert Zion, in *Small Urban Spaces.*

"Violating all of the traditional minimum size principles of recreation administrators, this tiny single house lot, 15 by 60 feet, has been converted into a successful play oasis. . . . In addition to conventional play equipment (slide and climber), the brick walls serve as climbers, and their maze effect also is for play."

Design for Play
Richard Dattner
New York, Van Nostrand Reinhold, 1969.
144 pp., 11¼ x 9", $13.50.

Written as a guide to playground design, this book provides sensible recreation alternatives to the "asphalt desert" play area concept.

"The criteria for design outlined here are based on the needs of all those who are involved with playgrounds—children, parents, community, and city administration—and on the lessons to be learned from the way children play in the streets of our cities, when they invent their own facilities and create their own play environment. The practical application of these criteria is illustrated and evaluated in the case history of a major playground and in a survey of creative play facilities in the United States and Europe.

"Also discussed are a variety of neglected opportunities for play facilities, including rooftops, sidewalks, and barges."

The Camden adventure playground in London.

"A playground should present a variety of challenges ranging from things young children can master to things that require the skill and agility of older children. The structures in this playground can be used in many ways and at many levels. The cargo net is one route for scaling the low tower; ropes and timbers provide other approaches. The discarded cable spools can be used for climbing and rolling or as tables."

Richard Dattner's "Adventure Playground" in New York City's Central Park.

"The concept that provided the basis of the design was that of a group of small, varied and related elements surrounding a large central space. This would allow a child to choose among a number of different activities and places while feeling always that he was part of a larger group. The different elements were linked together to permit movement from one to another and to enclose the central space to which all related. The linked structures thus form a sort of wall that defines the physical boundaries of the children's area. In their variety of size and function, these structures offer a full range of choice— from quiet, individual play to active undertakings involving groups of children, and from simple activities to more complex ones by a series of manageable steps."

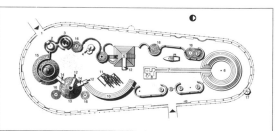

Painted waste-cans in the St. Barnabas House playground, New York City, Robert Nichols, architect.

Adventure Playgrounds

The adventure playground adds an additional element to our idea of recreation: the "build-it-yourself" concept of creating and shaping your own environment. Most urban recreation space merely exists to be played on. You can affect your environment by changing your relationship to it, by moving over, on, under or through things but often you cannot really change its shape or layout. Adventure playgrounds provide materials and space for participants to build their own, be it camp house, climbing structure, swings, tree house, or multiple-use sculpture. Materials are cheap and fairly easy to obtain. The basic activity is construction, with so many variations that adventure playgrounds can accommodate a wide age range (4-16 years old).

Materials:
timber
telephone poles
cargo nets
canvas sheets, scrap
corrugated tin sheets
cardboard boxes
wallpaper sheets
building excavation material
marble doorsteps
sinks and fixtures
door and window frames
car and truck tires
barrels and sewer pipes
ropes
telephone wire reels
tree stumps
bricks and cinderblocks
sand.

Adventure playgrounds are extensively discussed in *Small Urban Spaces, Environmental Planning for Children's Play, Play and Playgrounds,* and *Design for Play.*

Salvage Playgrounds

Another playground type which utilizes activities and material from the street is the salvage playground. The salvage playground uses standard equipment like slides or rubber tire swings interspersed with material of former industrial use: stripped jet planes, old fire engines, rowboats and dories, cars or buses stripped of engines, and even painted iron lungs. Activity centers around games played on the equipment. Salvage playgrounds are discussed in *Play and Playgrounds* and *Design for Play.*

Play and Interplay

M. Paul Friedberg, with Ellen Perry Berkeley
New York, Macmillan, 1970.
192 pp., 7¾x10½", $9.95.

This book attempts to redefine urban recreational planning in terms of users' "needs" rather than the traditional "facility development." Friedberg explores the activities of specific recreational groups—children's adventure play and what defines it, the elderly and their need for companionship—and concepts of recreational space in general. He suggests that by defining what people want to do, urban space can be designed to conform better to their needs. The book includes some specific design solutions from Friedberg's projects: the modular vest-pocket park, urban playgrounds, pedestrian plazas, and recreation waterfronts.

"The challenge in our urban environment is to use our resources to open recreational possibilities that are truly re-creational, that heighten experience and increase enjoyment for all urban dwellers and for all their lives."

M. Paul Friedberg's office designed a modular system of play equipment that can be erected quickly, used for the available period of time, and then broken down and returned to an equipment stockpile for re-use at another site. The system utilizes four different sets of materials: pipe and cable, steel tubing, bolted timbers, and precast concrete.

Each system was designed to provide play opportunities in itself (things to climb over, crawl through, hang from, etc.). Once erected, the equipment had to absorb all activity stresses without footings in order to be easily demountable and at the same time sturdy enough.

"The module is a starting point, very much like the architect starts with a single brick, and the playground form is produced by attaching the modules to each other. Facilities such as slides, swings, balancing boards, springboards, slide poles and so forth are but a single experience within the total form."

"Our new consciousness reveals the need for all of us to participate and contribute to our environment—not just experience it."

"Playgrounds are, like the rest of our society, compartmentalized. . . . Culturally, we separate man from his body, from his physical environment, from his social context. . . . I suggest that it is imperative to put play in context. To be understood in terms of the totality of urban life, of its congruence and equality with other aspects of human experience. . . . Until we can define the purpose and function of play and establish its validity within the urban context, it is an exercise in futility to analyze existing recreational systems, traditional or contemporary, in light of what we consider human needs."

Vest-Pocket Parks

Vest-pocket parks can happen in almost any kind of space, be it vacant lots in residential neighborhoods or commercial downtown areas. They can be as small as 15 by 60 feet accommodating such leisure activities as sitting, talking, watching, or reading. Or they may include several lots and contain a basketball or volleyball court, play equipment, fountains, sitting areas, and gardens.

The concept of the vest-pocket park developed from the "neighborhood commons" idea of Karl Linn and the work he did in Washington and Philadelphia during the 1950's. Today it is as much an economic and political tool as a physical one. It simply utilizes leftover land in dense residential areas for the two age groups that have the least mobility in the community, the very young (up to the age where they can cross the streets alone) and the very old.

Play and Playgrounds

Jeannette Galambos Stone and Nancy Rudolph
Washington, D.C., National Association for the
Education of Young Children, 1970.
72 pp., 10x13″.

Written as a report for the NAEYC, the book is a
picture guide through playgrounds and forms
of play.

*"We began simply by studying children as they
used space and materials in their play. But as we
progressed and our insights sharpened, we
found increasingly that we could not separate
the concepts of learning-through-play from the
life-styles of whole neighborhoods. And so we
came to feel that to treat playgrounds as separate entities, unrelated to anything else in the
community, is to repeat the mistakes of a
generation now past."*

Environmental Planning for Children's Play

Arvid Bengtsson
New York, Praeger, 1970.
224 pp., 8½x12″, $17.50.

This is a comprehensive survey of design solu-
tions for environmental play areas in the United
States, Canada, the European countries, and
Japan.

*"Among topics treated are climate, housing,
redevelopment of old areas, portable playgrounds,
gardens, zoos, various types of play (sand,
water, adventure), festivals, streets, malls, and
play areas for adults as well as children."*

Numerous photographs, sketches, and site plans
provide an articulate and coherent overview of
process and product in the development of
recreational facilities.

Our Man-Made Environment, Book 7

Alan Levy, William B. Chapman, Richard Saul
Wurman
Philadelphia, Group for Environmental
Education, 1970.
80 pp. plus 10 diecut sheets, 11½x9½″, price
varies from $4.95 each plus postage for 1 to 4
copies to $1.50 each plus postage for 25 or more
copies.

*"This book is an introduction to the study of the
man-made environment, of how our lives are
affected by our surroundings, of what we want
from them, and of how we can change them to
meet our needs.*

*"It is organized as a series of problems in response
to basic questions:*
1. What is the man-made environment?
2. Why do we build it?
3. What are the factors that influence it?
4. How do we change it?"

*"Children, of course, make
their own playgrounds every-
where. They practice stunts
and use their physical prow-
ess in throwing and jumping
rituals. . . . They thrust ahead
in improvisations of running
and hiding, skipping and
chanting, playing ball and
chalk games in the street,
balancing, climbing trees and
telephone poles, or putting
together a dollhouse or club-
house from cloth and sticks in
the back yard. They try out
new ideas, establish rules,
discuss ways and means,
try, fail, try again."*

Fulton Mall, Fresno, California, a former shopping
street converted into a
pedestrian mall.

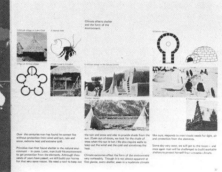

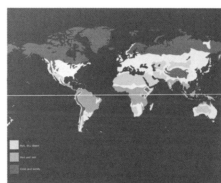

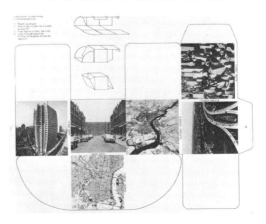

A typical spread and die-cut
page from *Our Man-Made
Environment, Book 7.*

Interplay

Bernard DeKoven
Philadelphia, School District of Philadelphia, 1972.
Four volumes plus manual, 3¾x6⅛″, $6.00.

This children's games catalogue, developed at the Intensive Learning Center in Philadelphia, is based on original research of games that children play. *"Its purpose is to guide children in their playing so that they can learn to work together and to help each other learn."*

It is a collection of indoor and outdoor games published in four volumes: *Locating, Adjusting, Expressing,* and *Relating.* The games involve both physical and mental skill development and dexterity. The manual was designed for both classroom and home use as an ongoing educational tool and is available through the Intensive Learning Center of the Philadelphia School System.

Additional Resources
American Society of Landscape Architects
1750 Old Meadow Rd.
McLean, Va.
Can provide playground information and the names of designers in any section of the country.

National Association for the Education of Young Children
1834 Connecticut Ave., N.W.
Washington, D.C.
Has produced many publications on play and playgrounds.

National Recreation and Park Association
1601 North Kent St.
Arlington, Va.
A source of sources, furnishing lists of publications about playgrounds.

Projects for Urban Spaces
Design Quarterly 77
Design Quarterly
807 Hennepin Ave.
Minneapolis, Minn. 55403

For specific information on campgrounds, lodging, and fees, write directly to the superintendent of the park or to
National Park Service
Room 1013
U.S. Dept. of the Interior
Washington, D.C. 20240

Detailed maps, brochures, and campground directories are available for most national forest areas. You may write to the
Forest Service
U.S. Dept. of Agriculture
Washington, D.C. 20250

The material for these games was researched by Bernard DeKoven, author of *Interplay* and director of Anyman, Inc.

The Street

"Enough cannot be said about the open space, the space one does not build on. . . . Why not deal in what a street really should be? I try to define streets as being rivers, which need docks, which need wharves. . . .

"A street is a community place . . . It's one of the first of our institutions. The walls of the houses that adjoin it are the walls of a community room."
Louis I. Kahn, 1972.

The New York City Department of Traffic found in a study that only one in four streets in the Bedford-Stuyvesant section of Brooklyn was used for traffic.

A plan was developed by I. M. Pei and partners and M. Paul Friedberg and Associates to convert the parallel parking to diagonal parking at both ends of the street and use the newly opened space in the middle for a park 75 by 200 feet.

"The park contains a fountain in which water cascades from a pedestal to a trough at the base of a wall, terminating at a still pool where children play. Children also have access to a tubular steel play frame with slides, swings and colored plaques. Three large honey locusts canopy a sitting area."
Design Quarterly 77

Architect Richard Dattner of New York City has developed a proposal for utilizing sidewalks and street space that is usually wasted to create small play nodes in residential sections.

"The sidewalks are widened at intersections and at fire hydrants in the middle of the block, where parking is prohibited. The paving between the curbs is painted in bright stripes to alert motorists. This kind of play area serves a number of functions, does not require buying costly land, is indestructible and safe, and is inexpensive enough to be built on almost every block in the city."

Low concrete benches form a protected area, shaded by trees where mothers can sit while children play. (The benches should be high enough to prevent infants from climbing over.) Sand is used within the areas ringed by benches, brick in the space between them.

In addition to using parts of the street and adjacent areas as play space, the street can be closed completely to traffic either temporarily or permanently and the area formally turned into recreation space.

In New York City, for example, the Police Athletic League closes streets at stated times for games of volleyball, basketball, music programs, and storytelling. During hot weather, fire hydrants are sometimes fitted with sprays for water play.

Designer Michael Alrschuler has proposed a plan for a play street to be used in conjunction with a storefront. The storefront provides storage for play and construction materials, office space for supervisory staff, and indoor play facilities in bad weather.

Both ideas are described in *Design for Play.*

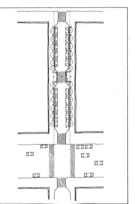
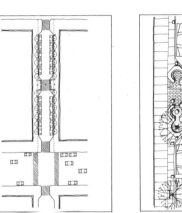

A Game Glossary

The material for these games was researched by Bernard DeKoven, author of *Interplay* and director of Anyman, Inc.

Ladder Hopscotch

Players use a court with narrow ladder rungs so players will hop sideways.

Encourage players to hop up the ladder on the right foot and back down on the left.

As many as four or five players can participate at once. Playing procedure:

1. Players hop in each space going up and down.

2. Players hop in every other space going up and down.

3. Players continue hopping and add one more space between hops each time a successful trip is made.

4. When a player has skipped four spaces between hops he changes to jumping between spaces.

5. A player who can skip the most spaces without missing wins.

A player misses if he steps on a line or touches the ground with any part of his body except his hopping foot.

When a player misses, he starts again at the step where the miss has occurred on his next turn.

Eleanor came from over the sea.
She don't dig no boys in dungarees.
When she's up she's up,
When she's down she's down.
Don't mess with her
When she's all around.
You go zee, zee, zee, number 10,
9, 8, 7, 6, 5, 4, 3, 2, 1

Hey, Mr. Bee
Bopity bop,

You sure look sweet,
Bopity bop.

Now let's get together with the feet.
You sure got together with the feet.
Now, let's get together with the hands.
You sure got together with the hands.
Now, let's get together with the hips.
You sure got together with the hips.
Now let's get together with the eyes.
You sure got together with the eyes.
Now, let's get together with the number five.

Circle Tops

Each boy has two tops. At first, all participants throw their tops (only one of them) into a circle about ten feet in diameter. They then throw the other top, the shooter, into the circle, trying to knock out the remaining tops. Any tops shoved out of the circle belong to the boy whose top did the shoving. Usually, the shooter must stay in the circle for the duration. This game is almost identical to marbles.

Step Ball

The players throw a small rubber ball against the steps, trying to catch it on the rebound. Each step has a different value, and usually most points are scored for bouncing the ball off the highest step. If a ball hits properly, it should strike one step and then the wall of the step above it. The player can compete against himself or with as many other players as the space can accommodate.

Tin Can Tommy

A small center area (about 5′ in diameter) is identified in the middle of the playing area. One player places a large empty can in the center of the circle. The group stands near him. He then throws the can as far as he can and begins to walk backward to retrieve the can. As he does so, the other players run and hide. He replaces the can and begins to search for the other players.

When he sees a player, he must run back to the can, place his foot on it, and call out the name of the player he saw. That player must join him in the circle. While the seeker is looking for other players, any player may try to free the prisoner(s) by kicking the can out of the circle. The prisoners, of course, may not touch the can. If the can is kicked out, the seeker cannot continue the search until he has replaced the can in the circle. Since he loses all power when the can is out of its place, all captives are freed. If the seeker makes a mistake and calls someone he didn't see, all players shout, "False Alarm," and the game begins again. The game continues until everyone has been caught.

Keepa, calla, balla,
Be on time.
School bell rings
a quarter to nine.
One, two, three of nine.
One, two, three of nine.

Here we go zoo-d-o, zoo-d-o, zoo-d-o,
Here we go zoo-d-o, all night long.
So, step back Sally, Sally, Sally
Walking through the alley all night long.
I looked through the alley and what did I see?
I saw a big fat Turkey from Tennessee.
I went way back
With a hump in my back.
Do the camel walk.
Do the camel walk

Duck-Duck Goose

Players sit in a circle. One walks around the outside of the circle tapping every player on the head, saying "Duck". When the player locates someone he wants to chase him, he says, "Goose". The goose tries to tag the other player. He tries to occupy the goose's seat. If the goose tags the player he must start over and find another goose. (Limit to three tries.) If the player succeeds in getting the goose's seat first, the goose is now "It".

Eena, leena, dissa leena, oo, ahh, ahh, beleena.
Achikachi, liberace, I love you, two-two, shampoo
Saw you with your boy friend
Last night.
What's his name?
Sammy White
How do you know it?
Peep through the key hole
noozey
Jumped out the window
Crazy

Wallball

This game is played by one to twelve, and sometimes more players. The object of the game is for one player to bounce a ball against a wall, and for another to retrieve the ball before it bounces on the sidewalk more than once. If the wall has lines on it, fair and foul areas are established. In some cases, the players must bounce the ball back without catching it. The rules for the game can get quite complicated. Basically a point is given to any player who misses. If that player accumulates a certain number of points, he is eliminated. An order is usually designated and players take turns accordingly.

Game Spaces

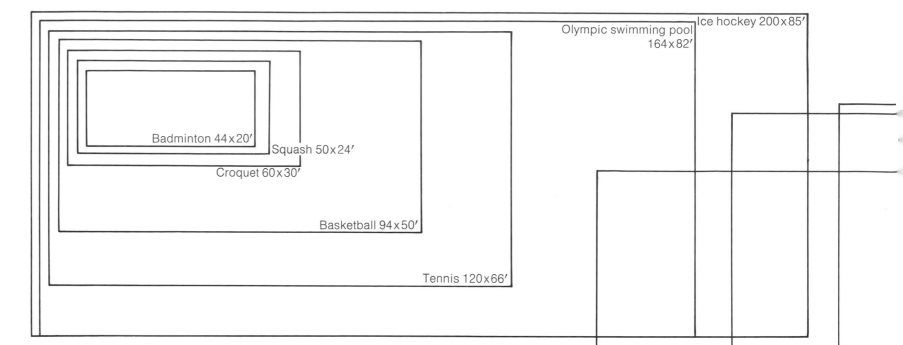

Olympic swimming pool 164 x 82'

Ice hockey 200 x 85'

Badminton 44 x 20'

Squash 50 x 24'

Croquet 60 x 30'

Basketball 94 x 50'

Tennis 120 x 66'

In one hour you could play
4½ holes of golf
½ game of baseball
at least 1 game of basketball
½ game of football
⅔ game of hockey
1 game of lacrosse
⅗ game of soccer

And in one hour you could probably
Walk three to four miles
Jog about five miles
Back-pack 2½ to three miles
Horseback ride about seven miles
Run eight miles
Bicycle about 15 miles
Ride a motorcycle 60 miles
Scull five miles

The scale of these drawings is the same as the scale of the spaces on pages 60-64 and the punch-outs, 1" = 25'. If the punch-outs don't give you the playing space you want for a particular game, you could measure from these pages and make your own label at the correct scale.

☐ Chess 2 x 2'

Bocce 62 x 18'

Horseshoes 50 x 10'

Billiards 10 x 5'

Curling 165 x 25'

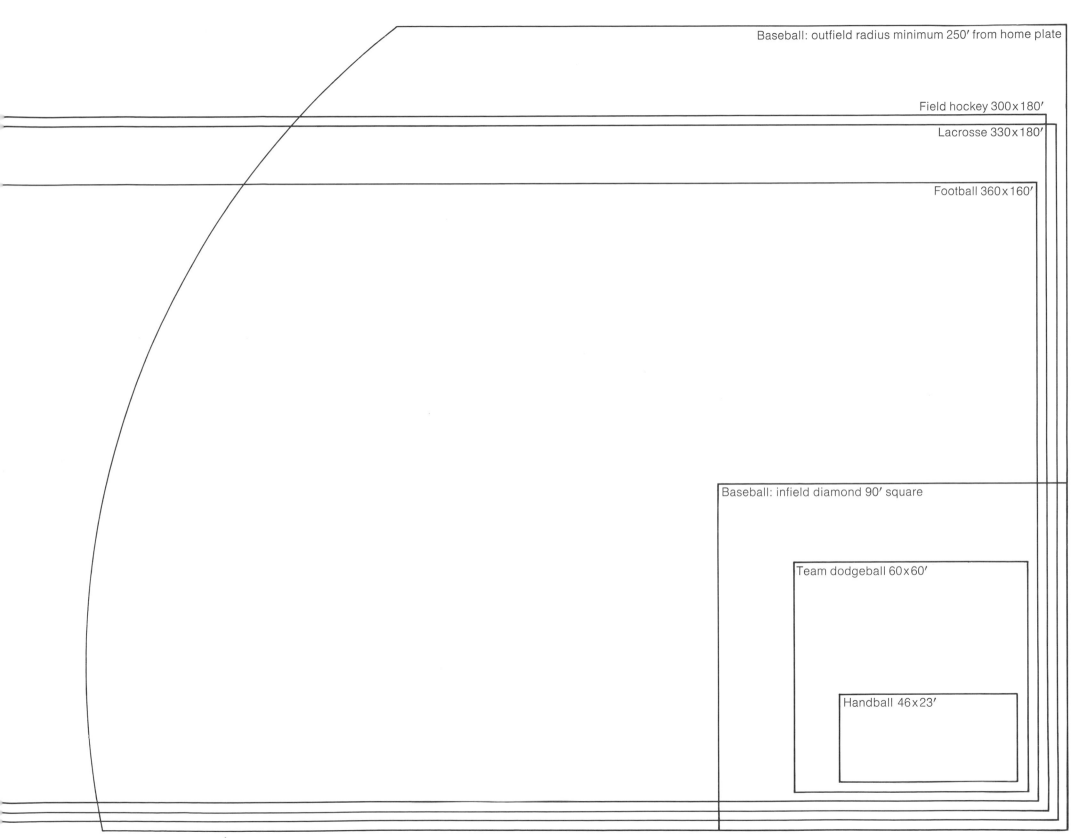

Baseball: outfield radius minimum 250' from home plate

Field hockey 300×180'

Lacrosse 330×180'

Football 360×160'

Baseball: infield diamond 90' square

Team dodgeball 60×60'

Handball 46×23'

Credits and Acknowledgments

Richard Saul Wurman, Alan Levy, and Joel Katz are members of the firm of Murphy Levy Wurman, Architecture and Urban Planning, and of GEE! Group for Environmental Education Inc., in Philadelphia.

Richard Saul Wurman, an architect, is the recipient of Guggenheim, Graham, and Chandler Fellowships, and the holder of many faculty positions, including Cambridge and Princeton Universities and City College of New York. He is on the board of the International Design Conference in Aspen and is a member of the task force and co-program chairman of the First Federal Design Assembly.

Alan Levy, architect, is the president of GEE! He is the recipient of the Brunner and Woodman Fellowships and has been on the architecture faculty of the University of Pennsylvania.

Joel Katz, writer, photographer, and graphic designer, is the recipient of Yale's Strong Prize for American Literature. He has taught at Yale and the Rhode Island School of Design and is currently on the faculty of the Philadelphia College of Art. His photographs have been exhibited and published both in this country and in Europe.

GEE! Group for Environmental Education Inc., is a non-profit corporation engaged in developing new ways of learning about our man-made environment. Recent GEE! publications, all distributed by The MIT Press, include:
Our Man-Made Made Environment, Book 7
The Process of Choice
Making the City Observable
Yellow Pages of Learning Resources
Aspen Visible
Man-Made Philadelphia
and also published by The MIT Press:
Urban Atlas: Twenty American Cities.

An undertaking of the breadth and complexity of *The Nature of Recreation* depends for its success on the assistance of many people. Specific thanks are due the people whose names follow.

Jean McClintock, of The Olmsted Sesquicentennial Committee, assisted in the selection of the Olmsted quotes, as well as contributing freely her knowledge of Olmsted's work and intentions.

Howard Brunner, of Murphy Levy Wurman, acted as picture editor as well as photographer throughout the process and problems of production.

Jan Frankina assisted with the appendix and marginal information. Scott Miller produced the illustrations. Both are members of Murphy Levy Wurman.

The inevitable uneven terrain in the manuscript was made plain with the help of Judy McCann of The MIT Press. David Scott and Jane Loeffler of the National Gallery of Art were helpful with their suggestions for our Introduction and Olmsted biography.

We must thank also William Alex and Elliot Willensky of The Olmsted Sesquicentennial Committee for making the Committee's rich store of images from Olmsted's day available to us.

Finally, special thanks to Wilder Green, of The American Federation of Arts, who kept a paternal and encouraging eye on our work throughout.

The inside covers are from *Central Park Country: A Tune Within Us,* by Mireille Johnston, with photographs by Nancy and Retta Johnston, a Sierra Club-Ballantine Book, reproduced by permission of the Sierra Club and Ballantine Books.

The Olmsted plans and engravings are from the Olmsted Office portfolio, Brookline, Massachusetts.

The nineteenth century views on pages 15, 16, 21 bottom left, 24, 25, 30 upper right, and 31 bottom middle, are from the collection of the Library of Congress.

Pages 3 and 21, skaters, Winslow Homer: *Skating of the Ladies, Central Park,* wood engraving. Metropolitan Museum of Art, New York, Harris Brisbane Dick Fund, 1928.

Page 6, photograph by H. N. Tieman, about 1890. Courtesy of the New York Historical Society, New York.

Page 11, photograph by Jacob A. Riis of the Henry Street Settlement, about 1898. The Jacob A. Riis Collection, Museum of the City of New York.

Page 13 left, second from top, from *Le Bouclier Arverne,* an adventure of Asterix the Gaul, by Uderzo and Goscinny (Dargaud).

Page 13 left, bottom, photograph by Arthur Griffin, from *Village Greens of New England,* by Louise Andrews Kent (Barrows).

Page 15, tree drawing by Jacques Hnizdovsky, from *Tree Trails in Central Park,* by M. M. Graff (New York, Greensward Foundation, 1970).

Page 22 middle left, Eileen Christelow.

Page 23 top right, *The Philadelphia Inquirer.*

Page 23 bottom right, detail from *Central Park—Summer,* a colored lithograph by John Bachmann, 1865. The J. Clarence Davies Collection, Museum of the City of New York.

Page 27 upper middle, Linn Giesler.

Page 29 upper right, National Parks Service.

Pages 30-31, aerial photograph by Aero Service Division of Litton Industries.

Pages 36-37 map, courtesy of Ken Fitzgerald and *Central Park: A History and a Guide,* by Henry Hope Reed and Sophia Duckworth (Clarkson N. Potter Inc.).

Page 46 upper right, Richard Saul Wurman.

Page 49, Nathaniel Lieberman/Todd A. Watts.

In the Appendix, the illustrations are taken from the books they accompany, except: page 69 top and page 71 right, from *Design for Play;* page 69 bottom, from *Forum;* page 71 middle, from *Design Quarterly 77.*

All other photographs, including the cover, are by Joel Katz or Howard Brunner.

Typesetting
Leon Segal Typesetting
Printing
Eugene Feldman, The Falcon Press
Paper
Wilcox Walter Furlong Mystery Opaque Smooth text, 80 lb.
Mead Black and White Offset Enamel cover, 80 lb.
International Springhill Index, 90 lb.
Champion Carnival Kraft olive, 24 lb.
Binding
Bless Bindery Company

2919